A BLUEPRINT FOR THE COMING ARMAGEDDON

Few people today doubt that history is moving toward some sort of climactic catastrophe. As I have discussed in previous books, current events are moving toward a showdown between the major world powers. Many secular scientists, statesmen and military experts believe that the world is heading for a global holocaust, involving an all-out nuclear war. The only variable with most of these experts is *when*.

No one who takes seriously these terrible and momentous events that are soon to come upon our world can fail to feel an overwhelming sense of burden. As I wrote these things, my heart literally cried out for a sure hope. I realized that these things will almost certainly fall upon my loved ones—unless . . .

THE RAPTURE

TRUTH OR CONSEQUENCES

HAL LINDSEY

BANTAM BOOKS

TORONTO • NEW YORK • LONDON • SYDNEY • AUCKLAND

THE RAPTURE: TRUTH OR CONSEQUENCES

Bantam Trade edition / August 1983
Bantam paperback edition / August 1985

Library of Congress Cataloging in Publication Data

Lindsey, Hal.
The rapture.

1. Rapture (Christian eschatology). 2. Eschatology.
3. Bible—Prophecies. I. Title.
BT887.L56 1983   236   82-45959

ISBN 0-553-24301-2

Published simultaneously in the United States and Canada

Bantam Books are published by Bantam Books, Inc. Its trade-
mark, consisting of the words "Bantam Books" and the por-
trayal of a rooster, is Registered in the United States Patent and Trademark
Office and in other countries. Marca Registrada. Bantam Books, Inc., The
Tishman Building, Fifth Avenue, New York, New York 10103.

PRINTED IN THE UNITED STATES OF AMERICA

O   0 9 8 7 6 5 4 3 2 1

ACKNOWLEDGMENT

I wish to thank Sondra Hirsch, a true daughter of Abraham, Isaac, and Jacob, for her tireless and dedicated help in typing this manuscript.

CONTENTS

ONE

A BLUEPRINT OF TOMORROW'S HISTORY

Few people today doubt that history is moving toward some sort of climactic catastrophe. As I have discussed in previous books,[1] current events are moving toward a showdown between the major world powers. Many secular scientists, statesmen, and military experts believe that the world is heading for a global holocaust, involving an all-out nuclear war. The only variable with most of these experts is *when*.

Of far greater significance is the fact that all the predicted signs that set up the final fateful period immediately preceding the second coming of Christ are now before us. We are on the verge of this period, which will last seven years. Students of prophecy have commonly called this time "the Tribulation" because of its awful worldwide judgments. Though the term "Tribulation" may not be the best, I'll use it for the sake of easy identification.

[1] *The Late Great Planet Earth, There's a New World Coming,* and *The 1980's: Countdown to Armageddon,* all published by Bantam Books, New York.

There is more prophecy pertaining to these seven years than any other comparable time period with which the Bible deals. Moses, Isaiah, Jeremiah, Ezekiel, Daniel, Zechariah, most of the so-called minor prophets, as well as almost the entire book of Revelation, prophesy about this period. The Tribulation is also the topic of Jesus' most extensive prophetic discourse (see Matthew 24 and 25; Mark 13; Luke 21:5-36).

The sheer volume of prophecy devoted to the Tribulation shows how important it is to God. Since we live in the general time of its occurrence, it is of immense importance to know what the Bible says will happen.

In this chapter I'm going to seek to arrange the events of the Tribulation in chronological order. I approach this task with a true sense of humility and reliance upon God's Spirit, for it is the most demanding of all Biblical interpretation. What is summarized here represents hundreds of hours of my own study over a period of twenty-six years, as well as the work of a number of other Biblical scholars.

The Duration of the Tribulation

The prophet Daniel gave the framework for the Tribulation era in Daniel 9:24-27. He was given a revelation concerning the main course of Israel's future. God decreed that seventy weeks of years[2] were allotted to the people of Israel. (One "week" of years equals seven years, so seventy weeks of years would be 490 years.) The prophecy is specifically concerned with the future of the Israelites and the city of Jerusalem (Daniel 9:24).

[2]Israel reckoned time in weeks of years as well as weeks of days (Leviticus 25:1-7). The context of this prophecy is that Israel was put in exile for failure to keep seventy Sabbatical years (2 Chronicles 36:15-23).

God's Prophetic Stopwatch

Around 530 B.C. Daniel prophesied that Israel's allotted time would begin with a decree to restore and rebuild the city of Jerusalem. This decree was given by Artaxerxes Longimanus of Persia in 444 B.C. Imagine that God had a great stopwatch with 490 years on it. He started the watch counting down the allotted time the day Artaxerxes signed the decree.

Daniel predicted that from the giving of this decree until Messiah the Prince appeared would be sixty-nine weeks of years, or 483 Biblical years, each of which are 360 days long. Scholars[3] have carefully worked out the chronology from ancient records and found that exactly 173,880 days (that is, 483 x 360 days) later, Jesus of Nazareth allowed Himself, for the first time, to be publicly proclaimed Messiah and heir to the throne of David (Luke 19:29–44).

Two Critical Historical Events

The prophecy then forecast that two historical events would take place *after* the 483 years, but *before* the final seven allotted years. First, the Messiah would be "cut off" or killed, and have nothing that was due Him as the heir to David's throne. Second, the city of Jerusalem and the temple, which was rebuilt by the Jews who had returned from Babylonian exile, would both be destroyed.

Jesus was crucified five days after being publicly presented as Messiah, and Jerusalem and the temple were destroyed some thirty-seven years later by Titus of Rome in A.D. 70.

God obviously stopped "the prophetic stopwatch" after it had ticked off 483 years. The predicted destruc-

[3]Sir Robert Anderson, *The Coming Prince* (Grand Rapids, Michigan: Kregel, 1975).

tion of Jerusalem happened far outside the predicted bounds of the last remaining week of years, so the clock could not have just continued ticking consecutively.

Because Israel failed to accept her Messiah and instead "cut him off" by crucifying him, God stopped the count-down seven years short of completion. During the ensu-ing parenthesis in time, God turned His focus to the Gentiles and created the Church.

The Last Week

It is the remaining seven years of this prophecy that shed so much light upon the Tribulation period. Daniel Chapter 9, Verse 27 tells us the following:

(1) The final seven years, or the Seventieth Week of Daniel as some call it, begins with the sign-ing of a protective treaty between Israel and the Antichrist, who will come from the revived Ro-man Empire (9:27) composed of ten European nations.

(2) There will apparently be a temple rebuilt shortly before or at this time, because sacrifice and offerings will be resumed. Jews wishing to return to this type of observance of Mosaic law and worship could do so only in a temple re-built on its ancient site in old Jerusalem.

(3) After three and one-half years, the Roman Dic-tator will betray Israel and set up "The Abom-ination of Desolation." This refers to the desecration of the temple. The Antichrist will enter the holy of holies and will erect there a statue of himself, and proclaim himself to be God (Matthew 24:15; 2 Thessalonians 2:3–4; Revelation 13:14–15).

(4) Jesus, speaking of this event, warned that it signaled the beginning of the worst tribulation

ever seen on earth, which will continue for the remaining three and one-half years (Matthew 24:15–22).

(5) I have gone into some detail on Daniel 9:24–27 because it clearly illustrates that the final seven years, or the Seventieth Week, specifically pertains to God's unfinished business with the Israelite people and Jerusalem. It is a time when God's special focus is back on the Israelites as a people distinct from the Gentiles and the Church. It is an allotment of time in which Old Testament covenants to Israel are to be fulfilled and completed.

It therefore does not seem to be a time when the Church, with its distinct calling and purpose, could be present. For if the Church were present, there could be no distinction between Jew and Gentile as the following verses indicate are the rule for this present age:

"For by one Spirit we were all baptized into one body, whether Jews or Greeks, whether slaves or free, and we were all made to drink of one Spirit." (1 Corinthians 12:13)

"For there is no distinction between Jew and Greek; for the same Lord is Lord of all, abounding in riches for all who call upon Him;" (Romans 10:12)

"There is neither Jew nor Greek, there is neither slave nor free man, there is neither male nor female; for you are all one in Christ Jesus." (Galatians 3:28)

"—a renewal in which there is no distinction between Greek and Jew, circumcised and uncircumcised, barbarian, Scythian, slave and freeman, but Christ is all, and in all." (Colossians 3:11)

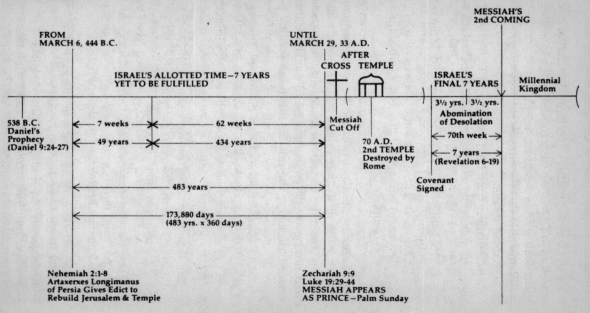

DANIEL'S PROPHECY OF 70 SABBATICAL YEARS
(Daniel 9:24-27)

MESSIAH'S
2nd COMING

FROM
MARCH 6, 444 B.C.

UNTIL
MARCH 29, 33 A.D.

AFTER
CROSS TEMPLE

ISRAEL'S ALLOTTED TIME—7 YEARS
YET TO BE FULFILLED

ISRAEL'S
FINAL 7 YEARS

Millennial
Kingdom

3½ yrs. | 3½ yrs.
Abomination
of Desolation

538 B.C.
Daniel's
Prophecy
(Daniel 9:24-27)

7 weeks → ← 62 weeks

Messiah
Cut Off

49 years → ← 434 years

70 A.D.
2nd TEMPLE
Destroyed by
Rome

← 70th week →
7 years
(Revelation 6-19)

483 years

Covenant
Signed

173,880 days
(483 yrs. x 360 days)

Nehemiah 2:1-8
Artaxerxes Longimanus
of Persia Gives Edict to
Rebuild Jerusalem & Temple

Zechariah 9:9
Luke 19:29-44
MESSIAH APPEARS
AS PRINCE — Palm Sunday

Yet in Daniel's prophecy about the Tribulation period, as well as in Revelation Chapters 6–18, the Israelites are again dealt with as a distinct, separate, and special people. Remember this very important point, for much will be said about it later.

To summarize, from the prophecy of Daniel 9:27, we know the following, as illustrated by the chart on page 6.

Now using this framework, I'm going to fit the many other prophecies together.

Events Just Before Tribulation

It is apparent that sometime before the seven-year Tribulation begins, the Antichrist will receive a mortal wound, be miraculously healed, be indwelt by Satan, and take over the ten nations of what we now know as the Common Market (Revelation 13:3). These things must first occur in order to give him the political position and power base from which to sign the protection treaty with Israel which officially begins the Tribulation.

A False Prophet, or pseudo-Messiah to Israel (Revelation 13:11–17), will be manifested before the Tribulation begins, for he is the leader of Israel who will make the covenant with the Roman Dictator (the Antichrist).

The great falling away or apostasy of the professing Christian Church also takes place before the beginning of the Tribulation which is sometimes called "the Day of the Lord" (2 Thessalonians 2:3).

The Tribulation Begins

When the Antichrist and the Israeli pseudo-Messiah sign the treaty of protection for Israel, the last seven years of Daniel's prophecy begins (Daniel 9:27 and 11:36–39). From that point final countdown resumes on God's prophetic stopwatch. There will be exactly 7 x 360 days, or 2,520 days, until the second coming of Jesus the Messiah.

In the beginning of this time frame, there will also occur the most important and incredible manifestation of God's grace for this period. One hundred and forty-four thousand Jews in Israel will be miraculously brought to faith in their true Messiah, the Lord Jesus. According to Revelation 7:1–4, this will occur before any harm comes upon the earth, the sea, or any vegetation. This means that the conversion must be right at the beginning of the Tribulation.

The context indicates that the evangelistic success of these elect and chosen people from the twelve tribes of Israel (excepting the tribe of Dan) will be awesome (Revelation 7:9-17).

Two Prophets that Shake the World

Revelation 11:3-13 traces the most unusual mission of two prophets. God sets them uniquely apart by calling them *"His* two witnesses" and by granting them *"His* own authority." I believe that these two will be none other than Moses and Elijah, who will be sent to prepare Israel for the true Messiah, and to expose the pseudo-Messiah. They will shake up not only Israel but the world for 1,260 days, or the first three and one-half years of the Tribulation.

Apparently the world at large will hate their message of warning and exposé, because all rejoice at their death.

The First Series of Judgments Begins

The first series of judgments to be unleashed on the world are called "the seven seals," and are recorded in the book of Revelation. These "seals" are fixed on a great scroll that contains God's decreed judgments. The scroll is progressively unrolled with the breaking of each seal.

THE FIRST SEAL—ANTICHRIST REVEALED

The first seal is broken at the beginning of the Tribulation. It releases the Antichrist of Rome to begin his mission of world conquest. He will bring all nations under his authority, using the European Common Market as his economic and political power base (Revelation 6:1–2; Daniel 8:23–25).[4]

General Conditions of the First Half of the Tribulation

The fear of war will apparently be stopped by the negotiating genius of the Roman Dictator. He will find solutions to such problems as the Soviet Union's desire for world conquest, the Sino–Soviet split, the enmity between the Arab and the Jew, the poverty-spawned revolutions of the third world, and the forthcoming international economic collapse.

Listen to what the Holy Spirit foretells the people of the world will say: "Who is like the beast [Antichrist], and who is able to wage war with him?" (Revelation 13:4). "While they are saying, 'Peace and Safety!'" (1 Thessalonians 5:3). In fact, Daniel shows that the Antichrist will use people's desire for peace to gain control of the world, "And through his [Antichrist] policy also he shall cause craft [deceit] to prosper in his hand; and he shall magnify *himself* in his heart, and *by means of peace* shall destroy many . . ." (Daniel 8:25, KJV).* This man will know how to use the world's desire for peace to his own diabolical ends. The Messiah-rejecting

[4] Hal Lindsey, *There's a New World Coming* (Eugene, Oregon: Harvest House, 1973), pp. 180–195; 228–249.

*Throughout the book, my emphases in quotes from Scripture are shown in **boldface italics**; *regular italics* show natural emphases; and amplified word or phrase meanings are set off by square [ ] brackets.

world will be given over to his deceptions as a Divine judgment (2 Thessalonians 2:9-12).

Persecution will begin to spread worldwide upon those who believe in the Messiah during this first half of Daniel's Seventieth Week. Many false teachers and prophets will arise, and millions of true believers will be massacred. The Antichrist's apostate world religion will apparently spearhead this persecution (see Matthew 24:9-14 and Revelation 17:14).

The Midpoint of the Tribulation

Many things begin to happen quickly as the midpoint of the Tribulation is reached. This very important time is signaled by a very specific event. In the middle of Daniel's Seventieth Week the Roman Dictator will break his covenant with the Israelis and stop the offering of sacrifices and temple worship. He will then desecrate the temple by entering the holy of holies and proclaiming himself to be God (2 Thessalonians 2:4).

This act is technically known in the Scripture as the "abomination of desolation." Jesus said that this would be the sign for believers living in Israel to flee to the mountains (Matthew 24:15-20) because this would be the beginning of unprecedented catastrophes. Listen to His warning,

"For then there will be a great tribulation, such as has not occurred since the beginning of the world until now, nor ever shall. And unless those days had been cut short, no life would have been saved; but for the sake of the elect, those days shall be cut short." (Matthew 24:21-22)

Jesus' warning for the believing Israelites to flee for protection coincides with the prophetic promise of protection in Revelation 12:6, 13-17.

"And the woman [Israel] fled into the wilderness where she had a place prepared by God, so that there she might be nourished for one thousand two hundred and sixty days [three and one-half years]."

"And when the dragon [Satan] saw that he was thrown down to the earth, he persecuted the woman who gave birth to the male child [Jesus]."

"And the two wings of the great eagle were given to the woman, in order that she might fly into the wilderness to her place, where she was nourished for a time [one year] and times [two years] and half a time [one-half year], from the presence of the serpent [Satan]."

"And the serpent poured water like a river out of his mouth [symbolic of invading armies of Ezekiel 38–39] after the woman, so that he might cause her to be swept away with the flood. And the earth helped the woman, and the earth opened its mouth [great earthquake] and drank up the river which the dragon poured out of his mouth."

Most believe that this place of protection for believing Israel will be the ancient fortress city of Petra, which is carved out of the rock of a protected canyon in southern Jordan.

THE SECOND SEAL OPENED—WAR BEGINS

Shortly after the "abomination of desolation," the second seal is opened, "and another, a red horse went out; and to him who sat on it, it was granted to take peace from earth, and that men should slay one another; and a great sword was given to him." (Revelation 6:4)

Up until this point, the Antichrist has kept a pseudo-peace going on earth. But now war begins and his careful alliances are shattered. The second seal unleashes the following:

First, the Arab armies led by Egypt launch an all-out attack against Israel (Daniel 11:40). This war will probably start over a dispute concerning Jerusalem (Zechariah 12:2–3).

Second, the Soviet Union and its allies seize upon this excuse and launch an all-out invasion of the Middle East by land, sea and air (Ezekiel 38:8–17; Daniel 11:40–41). The Soviets then continue through Israel into Egypt and take it over in a classic double cross. The Soviet commander will apparently plan to take over Africa as well (Daniel 11:42–43).

At this point the Soviet invasion is stopped. News from the north troubles the commander. As he looks northward from Egypt, he faces Western Europe and sees the mobilizing of the Western armies led by the ten-nation confederacy of the Common Market.

Also, the Russian leader is troubled by news from the east. The Oriental forces led by the People's Republic of China declare war on Russia and start their thrust toward the Middle East (Daniel 11:44; Revelation 16:12).

The Soviet army returns to Israel to make a stand against the combined Western and Eastern forces. It is here that the Soviets and their satellite countries will be annihilated (Daniel 11:45; Ezekiel 38 and 39; Joel 2:20).

All of this will take considerable time, perhaps months. In the same time frame the remaining seals of Revelation are opened.

THE THIRD SEAL—GLOBAL ECONOMIC CATASTROPHE

The opening of the third seal brings worldwide economic collapse. After war breaks out in the Middle East, oil from the Persian Gulf will be halted and worldwide economic chaos will set in. Food will become scarce and very expensive (Revelation 6:5–6).

THE FOURTH SEAL—ONE-FOURTH OF MANKIND PERISHES

The opening of the fourth seal brings death to one-fourth of the world's population. The enormity of this tragedy can hardly be imagined. In the space of a few months over one billion people will perish through war, famine, epidemics and breakdown of society (Revelation 6:7–8). All of these things will be the natural repercussions of the war in the Middle East.

THE FIFTH SEAL—MASSACRE OF SAINTS

The opening of the fifth seal unleashes a horrible persecution of believers. The Roman Antichrist and the Israeli False Prophet launch a wholesale slaughter of believers (Revelation 13:5–7). They have an ingenious method of exposing believers. The Antichrist and False Prophet use economics to achieve absolute control of the people. They will institute a monetary program by which every person in the world receives a number whose prefix is 666. This begins during the first half of the Tribulation. Without this number, no one is able to buy, sell or hold a job. But to get this number, a person has to swear allegiance to the Roman Antichrist. A true believer in the Messiah cannot do this, so he is exposed and has no means of survival (Revelation 13:13–18). The persecution which begins during the first half of the Tribulation (Matthew 24:9–13) now achieves full force. Computers have made it possible for the first time in history to do exactly what is predicted here. Plans are already being made for a cashless society in which all people will have credits electronically transferred by computer instead of currency.

THE SIXTH SEAL—FIRST NUCLEAR EXCHANGE

The opening of the sixth seal begins what all nations fear—nuclear war. Apparently warfare has been fought conventionally up until this point. But the Soviet leaders, in a desperate situation, decide to launch a first strike. Ezekiel 39:6 says that fire is unleashed upon Magog (the cryptic name for Russia) and the "coastlands," which in ancient times referred to the great, faraway Gentile civilizations. Today the term would mean "continents." I believe that this is forecasting a nuclear exchange between the Soviet Union, Europe, United States, and China.

The world is horrified, but the worst is yet to come.

THE SEVENTH SEAL—ANOTHER SERIES OF JUDGMENTS

The seventh seal is opened and there is a lull in judgment as God gives mankind a chance to repent. The seventh seal is actually the releasing of the seven trumpet judgments which are much more severe than the first six seals (Revelation 8:1-2). It is important to note that God gives a gracious interlude between each series of judgments, which shows His reluctance to pour out more of His wrath. But each series of judgments is more severe and seem to be timed more closely together.

With the sounding of the seven trumpets judgment greatly increases in speed, scope and severity.

THE TRUMPETS—A JUDGMENT OF THIRDS

The first trumpet brings a burning of one-third of the earth's surface, one-third of the trees, and all the grains and grasses on earth (Revelation 8:7). This could be caused by fire storms started by the numerous nuclear explosions of the sixth seal.

The second trumpet gives a *foreview* of a great nuclear naval battle. Convoys of merchant ships and warships are all destroyed. It appeared to the apostle John to be caused by a great burning mountain cast into the sea. I believe this is an excellent first-century description of a twentieth-century hydrogen bomb. A third of all ships and life in the sea is destroyed by this nuclear battle (8:8–9).

The third trumpet brings a poisoning of one-third of all the world's fresh water. This could be caused by another nuclear exchange resulting in fallout, which would poison the fresh water with radiation. The burning star or meteor hitting the earth (8:10) is a perfect description of ballistic missile warheads re-entering the atmosphere.

The fourth trumpet is a judgment against light reaching the earth. Light from the sun, moon and stars is diminished by one-third. I believe this is a result of the debris spread into the upper atmosphere by the blast of hundreds of nuclear warheads. This would block out light from space. Just imagine how this will add to the panic and terror already gripping the earth (8:12).

The fifth trumpet is very difficult to discern. Whatever it is, some very vicious demons who have been bound until that time will be closely involved. Unbelievers will be so tormented by this judgment that they will seek death but be unable to find it. This will last for five months (9:1–12). This could be the result of some form of biological warfare. The Soviet Union already has a formidable arsenal of chemical weapons that could easily produce the symptoms given here.

The sixth trumpet coincides with the prophecy of Daniel 11:44 where news from the east troubles the Soviet commander. The vast Chinese army and its Oriental allies mobilize to contest the Soviet invasion of the Middle East and Africa. The activity at the Euphrates River, which was the ancient boundary between east and west, indicates that the Oriental power is incited to war by some especially powerful and vicious demons who were bound there (9:13-14).

This army numbers two hundred million. Only China could raise such an army, and has already claimed that number of men under arms. As they move toward the Middle East, they wipe out **one third** of earth's population. They do this with fire and brimstone which again seems to indicate a massive use of nuclear weapons (9:15-18).

Can you imagine the horror of these times: With one-fourth of mankind killed by the fourth seal of judgment, and one-third killed by this one, it brings the total of the earth's population destroyed to one-half. And all of this occurs in a period of less than three years. No wonder Isaiah said of this time, "The inhabitants of the earth are burned, and few men are left." (Isaiah 24:6) And again, "I will make mortal man scarcer than the gold of Ophir. Therefore I shall make the heavens tremble, and the earth will be shaken from its place at the fury of the Lord of hosts." (Isaiah 13:12-13)

An Incredible Survey of World Opinion

As terrible as all this is, the real holocaust is yet to come. It staggers the imagination to consider the hardness of the human heart reflected in the Divine survey of mankind's attitude after all these judgments take place. But listen to the Holy Spirit's preview of the world's attitude, "And the rest of mankind, who were not killed by these plagues, did not repent of the works of their hands, so as not to worship demons, and the idols of gold and silver and of brass and of stone and of wood, which can neither see nor hear nor walk; and they did not repent of their murders nor of their immorality nor of their thefts." (Revelation 9:20–21)

It is important to note that the history of the Tribulation period recorded in Revelation unfolds chronologically with the three series of judgments. The seventh seal actually unleashes the seven trumpet judgments. The seventh trumpet unleashes the seven golden bowl judgments.

Interspersed between the three series of judgments, in typical ancient Hebrew style,* are many historical sketches of the main subjects who are the prime movers during the seven years of Tribulation. These masterfully written vignettes display the wisdom and genius of the Holy Spirit who inspired them. They sometimes reach far back into history to trace why certain things occur; or they will reach into future history to show their final outcome and influence on the other events of the Tribulation.

More will be said about the framework of the book of Revelation in a later chapter. Those who wish a full exposition of the Revelation may wish to read my book, *There's a New World Coming*.

The Seventh Trumpet—Bowl Judgments Unleashed

When the seventh trumpet sounds, it is very near the end of Daniel's Seventieth Week (Revelation 11:15). There is another gracious delay of events on earth before the judgments of the seventh trumpet strike. Mean-

*Note that the *style*, not the *language*, is Hebrew. The language of Revelation, like all of the New Testament, is Greek.

while, in heaven the Lord Jesus, the Messiah, proclaims his right to the title deed of the earth and inaugurates His kingdom.

Mankind is given one last chance to repent before the most horrible and extensive judgments of all time hit the earth. During this time Babylon, the great worldwide religious system ruled from Rome, is destroyed by the Antichrist and his ten-nation confederacy (see Revelation 17:16–18 and 18:1–24).

There are also two "reapings" of the earth at this time. The first is a great final evangelistic movement whose purpose is to bring the last group of souls to salvation. The second will bring the rest of the unbelieving world into a final great war whose vortex is centered near Jerusalem and throughout the Jordan Valley (Revelation 14:12–20).

Apparently all those who are going to believe in the Messiah have done so by this time. The choice of whether to receive or reject the 666 mark of allegiance to the Antichrist will have been made. Only someone who believes and understands the truth about Jesus and the Bible will have the reason and courage to stand up to the consequences of rejecting this mark. Those who do receive it cannot be saved (see Revelation 14:9–12). The die is cast. At this point, the eternal destiny of every living human being will already be determined by his own choice.

THE SEVEN GOLDEN BOWLS OF GOD'S WRATH

About these final judgments John the Apostle wrote, "And I saw another sign in heaven, great and marvelous, seven angels who had seven plagues, which are the last, because in them the wrath of God is finished . . . and one of the four living creatures gave to the seven angels seven golden bowls full of the wrath of God, who lives forever and ever." (Revelation 15:1–7)

These seven horrifying judgments are all predicted in the Sixteenth Chapter of Revelation. Whereas the previous judgments had some restraint, these are worldwide and unrestrained.

The first bowl brings cancer upon all those who have the 666 mark on them. This could be a natural aftermath from the radiation of so many nuclear explosions. It appears that God will Divinely protect the believers from this plague.

The second bowl turns the sea to blood and every living thing in the ocean dies.

The third bowl turns all fresh water on earth to blood.

The fourth bowl judgment intensifies the sun's rays causing horrible heat waves. This would happen when the ozone layer of the upper atmosphere is damaged by the nuclear warfare.

The fifth bowl brings a special judgment of thick darkness upon the throne of the Roman Dictator.

The sixth bowl is terrifying indeed. The mighty two-hundred-million-man Oriental army has now reached the Euphrates River, which has dried up so that their advance can be quickened. It seems that this army will also take advantage of the confusion caused by the darkness in the Antichrist's capital. Satan, the Antichrist, and the False Prophet use demonic power to deceive all the nations on earth to gather for a suicidal war. Since by this time the Soviet bloc will have destroyed the Arab armies, and the Soviets in turn will have been destroyed (Ezekiel 39:1–6; Daniel 11:45), the last battle will be fought between the Western armies and the Chinese-led Eastern army.

The vortex of this enormous battle will be fought at the place called in Hebrew *Har-Magedon* and in English *Armageddon*. This is the area around the ancient city of Meggido, which overlooks a great valley in northern Israel.

The Death of All Cities

The seventh bowl judgment seems to be primarily against cities. The greatest earthquake in the history of mankind occurs. Then *all* the cities of the Gentile nations are destroyed (Revelation 16:19). Apparently, the earthquake will affect the whole world. Just think of it. Cities like New York, London, Paris, Tokyo, and Mexico City, all destroyed. And remember, these are not cleverly devised myths we are talking about. Four-fifths of all Bible prophecy has been fulfilled in history. The last one-fifth relates to the end times and is beginning to fit into place. Even as I write these words I am overwhelmed by the horrors that will befall this unbelieving generation.

THE SECOND ADVENT OF THE MESSIAH

Shortly after the final bowl judgment, the personal, awesome return of Messiah Jesus, the Lord of Lords and King of Kings, begins. These are some of the characteristics of his return:

First, it will be **sudden and instantaneous**, "For just as lightning comes from the east, and flashes even to the west, so shall the coming of the Son of Man be." (Matthew 24:27)

Second, Jesus will personally return in bodily form, and will be visible to all the world,

"Then the sign of the Son of Man will appear in the sky, and then all the tribes of the earth will mourn, and they will see the Son of Man coming on the clouds of the sky with power and great glory." (Matthew 24:30)

*"Behold, he is coming with clouds, and **every eye** will see Him, even those who pierced Him; and all the*

tribes of the earth will mourn over Him." (Revelation 1:7)

Third, His return will be with **power** and **great glory**. Fourth, all people will **mourn** over Him, though for most of the survivors it is not in repentance. Hearts are so hardened by this point that the armies fighting each other join forces and try to prevent the Lord Jesus' return, "And I saw the beast [the Roman Antichrist] and the kings of the earth and their armies, assembled to make war against Him who sat upon the horse, and against His army." (Revelation 19:19) This reveals the incredible truth that these men hate the Lord even more than they hate each other. So, demonstrating hardened hearts beyond comprehension, they join forces and attack the Lord Himself.

Fifth, His return will be with **violent judgment** and devastating, unprecedented destruction of those who resist Him,

"For the Lord's indignation is against all the nations, and His wrath against all their armies; He has utterly destroyed them, He has given them over to slaughter." (Isaiah 34:2)

"For I will gather all the nations against Jerusalem to battle . . . then the Lord will go forth and fight against those nations, as when He fights on a day of battle." (Zechariah 14:2–3)

"And those slain by the Lord on that day shall be from one end of the earth to the other. They shall not be lamented, gathered, or buried; they shall be like dung on the face of the ground." (Jeremiah 25:33; see also Revelation 19:11–16)

Sixth, He will return with His bride, who is already prepared and adorned with her rewards,

> *"Let us rejoice and be glad and give glory to Him, for the marriage of the Lamb* **has come** *and His bride* **has made** *herself ready.' And it was given to her to clothe herself in fine linen, bright and clean; for the fine linen is the righteous acts of the saints.*

> *"And he said to me, 'Write, "Blessed are those who are invited to the marriage supper of the Lamb." ' And he said to me, 'These are the true words of God' . . . and I saw heaven opened; and behold, a white horse, and He who sat upon it is called Faithful and True; and in righteousness He judges and wages war . . . and the armies which are in heaven, clothed in fine linen, white and clean, were following Him on white horses."* (Revelation 19:7–9, 11, 14)

These verses clearly show that the bride of Christ, who is already judged and rewarded before the second advent, is also the army that comes with Him when He returns to judge the earth.

Remember this, for much more will be said about *who* this bride of Christ is, and *why* she is already in heaven and rewarded *before* the second advent of Jesus.

Seventh, He will return to set up the kingdom of God on earth. This kingdom was offered and rejected in His first coming, postponed during the present age, and to be set up at His second coming (Matthew 4:17, 23:37–39; Acts 1:6; Zechariah 14:9–21; Daniel 7:26–27; Revelation 19:11–20:6).

The Enormity of the Tragedy

At this point I feel it important to take stock of the enormous loss of life during the seven years of Daniel's Seventieth Week.

First, there will be many who will die during the persecution of believers in the first half of the Tribulation (Matthew 24:9–14).

Second, there will be a minimum of over one billion people killed under the judgment of the fourth seal (Revelation 6:7–8).

Third, there will be "a multitude of believers too great to be numbered" massacred during "the great Tribulation" of the last half of Daniel's Seventieth Week (Revelation 6:9–11 compared with 7:9–17). Since there are numbers like two hundred million used in Revelation, this must be an *enormous* group, too large to be numbered.

Fourth, one-third of the remaining population will die under the sixth trumpet judgment (Revelation 9:15). Assuming that the population of the earth at the beginning of the Tribulation will be about five billion, two billion five hundred million people will die in the fourth seal and sixth trumpet judgments alone.

Fifth, in the great worldwide destruction of cities that occurs during the seventh bowl judgment, many millions more will surely be killed.

Sixth, vast numbers around the whole world will die during the actual second coming of the Messiah according to Jeremiah 25:33 and other passages.

In summary, it would appear that those who survive would be not more than fifty million. No wonder God warned through the prophets about the end, "I will make mortal man scarcer than pure gold . . ." (Isaiah 13:12); "the inhabitants of the earth are burned, and few men are left . . ." (Isaiah 24:6); and Jesus Himself said,

"Unless those days are cut short, no life will be saved . . ." (Matthew 24:22).

Why have I gone into all this? Because I believe it is of utmost importance to squarely face exactly what the Scriptures predict about this period. Those who say that the believers in the Church are going to go through all these horrors never really bring out what that means. And no wonder. It's easy to see why they minimize these things, because against the backdrop of such terrifying events, it's rather difficult to get people excited about the nearness of Christ's return.

In the light of these prophecies, very few who begin the Tribulation would live to see His coming anyway. So how could anyone inspire the hope and comfort that is promised in Paul's teaching of Jesus' imminent return (1 Thessalonians 4:15-18)? Ladd, Gundry, and other post-Tribulationists talk about the hope being the prospect of seeing and being with the Lord in eternity. That is the hope normally promised to those who will die and be resurrected. But the Rapture is a hope presented to the living, not the dead. There is an enormous difference in the hope (if you can call it that) of the post-Tribulationists and the pre-Tribulationist hope presented around the mystery of the translation (Rapture) of **living saints.**

MEANWHILE, BACK AT THE END OF THE TWENTIETH CENTURY

I have endeavored to cover briefly the main events that take place during the Tribulation. Much prayer was offered as I sought to correlate important prophecies and arrange them in chronological order.

No one who takes seriously these terrible and momentous events that are soon to come upon our world can fail to feel an overwhelming sense of burden. As I wrote these things, my heart literally cried out for a sure hope. I realized that these things will almost certainly fall upon my loved ones—unless . . .

The rest of this book will deal with whether or not we have a real hope.

TWO

CLARIFYING THE ISSUE

I decided to write this book because I see a growing confusion and anxiety developing throughout the body of Christ worldwide. This confusion and anxiety comes from an uncertainty about whether the true Church, which is composed of all true believers in Jesus regardless of denomination, will go through the Tribulation, or through the first half of the Tribulation, or will be taken out of the world by Jesus before the Tribulation begins.

In my opinion, this question is about the most important one a Christian of this generation can ask. In all probability, most of the people reading this book will live to experience the answer.

About fifteen years ago this wouldn't have even been a question because most Christians didn't know much, if anything, about this issue. But since then there has been a flood of books, movies, teachers, and so forth, which have spread the message about the imminent return of the Lord Jesus, and the events that precede it.

Teaching about these end-time prophecies has lately been met with great interest around the world.

When I set out to do research for this book, I asked the Lord to overcome any prejudice or conditioning from the past, and to help me to be truly objective under the guidance of the Holy Spirit. My goal has not been to defend a view, but to seek the truth about *when* Christ is coming for His Church. I determined that if I should find that I had been wrong on this issue, that I would write a book acknowledging it.

I think it is important to bring out that as far as my own personal faith is concerned, if the Scriptures teach that the Church is to go through all or part of the Tribulation, I can certainly trust in God for His care and protection and press on. I want the truth, and I don't want to spread false hope; to be found a liar before God. That thought is more frightening to me than the Tribulation.

But, on the other hand, if Christ is coming *before* the Tribulation for His Church, this great hope should be shouted from the rooftops. As our world continues to move toward greater and greater peril, this hope will have an explosive effect upon believers. According to the Scripture, it will bring greater purity of life, comfort and peace in the midst of a turbulent world, and a bold witness for Christ.

In the months of study that followed, my main texts were the original languages of the Bible. However, I also read carefully the books of the major scholars representing the three different views about the time of Christ's coming for His Church. Many of these I had read before, but I wanted to make sure I had been fair with them.

At this point it is necessary to introduce a few important theological terms.

The coming of Christ for the Church in which He instantly catches up all living believers to meet Him in the air and translates them into immortal bodies without experiencing physical death is called the "Rapture" (1 Corinthians 15:51–54; 1 Thessalonians 4:15–18). The word *rapture* comes from a Latin translation of the Greek word *harpazo* in 1 Thessalonians 4:17 which is translated in English as "caught up." It literally means "to seize" or "to snatch away." If I had my way, I would call the Rapture "the great snatch."

All who interpret the Bible in a literal sense believe in the *fact* of the Rapture and that it is distinct from the second coming of Christ. The dispute is over exactly *when* the Rapture occurs in relation to the Tribulation period.

Those who believe that the Church will go through the entire Tribulation and be raptured simultaneously with Jesus' return to the earth in the second coming are called "post-Tribulationists."

Those who believe that the Church will go through the first half of the Tribulation, and will be raptured and taken to heaven at the midpoint of the Tribulation, are called "mid-Tribulationists."

Those who believe that the Church will be raptured before the Tribulation begins, to be with Christ in heaven and to return with Him at the end in the second coming are called "pre-Tribulationists."

I believe the following charts may help clarify the different views:

PRE-TRIBULATION RAPTURE

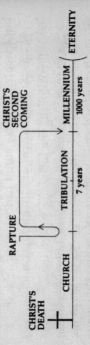

MID-TRIBULATION RAPTURE

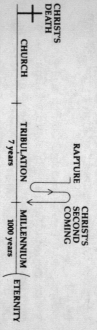

POST-TRIBULATION RAPTURE

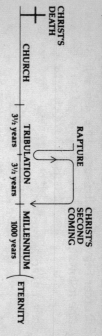

The New Protestant Purgatory

There is a fourth view concerning the Rapture of the Church which has recently been introduced. It is not widely taught, since it is unorthodox and at considerable variance with the Scripture. However, it is a view that could gain some following among those who are weak on knowledge of the Word of God and strong on experience and human viewpoint.

This view is in direct contradiction to one of the most central and important doctrines of all, that of salvation by grace through faith alone. It is commonly called the "Partial Rapture View."

There are some variations among its adherents, but generally it means the following: When the Lord Jesus comes to snatch away the true Church, only the spiritual believers will be taken. The carnal, or "back-slider" believers, will be left to go through the Tribulation. Most adherents of this view believe that the partial Rapture will occur before the Tribulation. This view is illustrated in the following chart:

PARTIAL RAPTURE THEORY

Why So Many Views?

Many, including myself, have puzzled over why there are so many conflicting views concerning a doctrine that is so important. This question becomes even more mystifying when you realize the kinds of people who are involved in the disagreement.

This has been especially hard for me, because many of those with whom I disagree on this issue are people I know and respect.

Some Areas of Common Agreement

This is the crux of the problem, that all the principal scholars and exponents of pre-, post-, and mid-Tribulationism are born again, love the Lord, believe the Bible is the Word of God, desire to teach the truth, and as far as I know live Godly lives.

Theologically, there is also a wide range of agreement. Almost all concerned hold to an orthodox view of the important central doctrines of the faith such as the person and work of Christ, justification by grace through faith, the inspiration of the Bible, and so forth.

In the field of prophecy (eschatology) there is general

agreement that there will be a literal seven years of world Tribulation, that Jesus will return visibly and personally, that He will then set up a literal 1,000-year earthly kingdom over which He will rule, that mortals will repopulate the earth, that there will be a final judgment at "the great white throne" at the end of the thousand years when all unbelievers of all ages past will be finally condemned, and that eternity begins after this.

In other words, what I've described above is a *premillennial view* of the Messiah's return and the Messianic kingdom. All the pre-, post-, and mid-Tribulationists are "premillennialists." Just so you'll know what this means, on the following page I have charted three views of the millennial kingdom.

Postmillennialists believe that the Church will overcome the world and bring the millennial period of peace and perfect environment to earth on its own. Then the Messiah will come at the end of history and receive the kingdom from the Church. This view flourished in the late nineteenth and early twentieth centuries, during a period of pseudo-optimism about the Church's missionary success and the effect of education on human nature.

But World War I seriously shook this view, and World War II all but wiped it out. It should be noted that the view is founded on a gross mishandling of the prophetic Scriptures. The allegorical method of interpretation is used throughout.

The term *"amillennial"* means no millennium, and proponents of this view believe there will be no specific period of Tribulation, no fulfillment of Daniel's prophecy about the Seventieth Week and no millennial kingdom. Jesus will simply come at the end of history, judge all people, believers and unbelievers, and start eternity.

The *only* way one can arrive at this view is by using an allegorical method of interpretation. This means that

PREMILLENNIAL VIEW

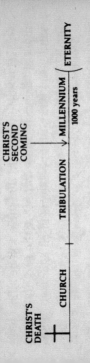

POSTMILLENNIAL VIEW

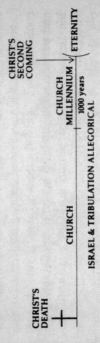

AMILLENNIAL VIEW

one assigns to words a meaning other than that normally understood and accepted at the time of writing.

Amillennialists concede that if prophecy is interpreted literally (normally), grammatically, and historically it will produce a premillennial view. The literal method allows for parable, allegory, and figures of speech, but recognizes that the context will clearly indicate when this is the case.

Amillennialism has some very dangerous side effects. First, it makes God guilty of not keeping unconditional covenants and promises made to the physical descendents of Abraham, Isaac, and Jacob, whom we call Jews today. For God not only swore that there would always be a distinct race of Israelites on earth, but that there will be a true believing remnant of Jews who will be established in a literal kingdom on earth ruled by the Messiah. If you look up the following verses you will see that the covenants depend upon God's faithfulness alone, not Israel's obedience:

(1) Promise of the land: Genesis 12:7; 13:15-16; 17:7-8.

(2) Promise of the land, a kingdom, and a greater Son of David (Messiah) as king: Psalm 89:27-37.

(3) Promise of restoration to the land of Israel from worldwide dispersion and establishment of Messiah's Kingdom: Jeremiah 31:31-37; Ezekiel 36, 37, 38, 39, and so forth.

(4) Promises that a remnant of the Israelites will be saved: Romans 11:25-29; Zechariah 13:8-9, Isaiah 10:20-22.

This is only a sampling of passages, but it shows how solemn God's covenants with the Israelites are. The restoration of the State of Israel in May 1948 is a literal confirmation of these promises.

Roots of Anti-Semitism

The second effect is that from the time that amillennialism began to be taught (about the fourth century, beginning with Augustine A.D. 345–430), it became a philosophical basis for anti-Semitism. Amillennialism teaches that the Church has been given the promises made to the Israelites because they crowned a history of unbelief by rejecting the Messiah. Therefore, since in this view the Israelites have no future in God's plan, and since they believe that "the Jews engineered the execution of Jesus," a subtle justification for the persecution of Jews resulted (Jeremiah 31:35–37).

There is evidence that this kind of thinking is reviving again today. There are those who are teaching that the State of Israel is filled with imposters and that there are no true Israelites today apart from spiritual Israel, which according to them is the Church.

This kind of teaching is demonic and heretical. I am thankful to say that no person who believes in the premillennial view can be anti-Semitic. In fact, the premillennialists are probably the truest non-Israelite friends the Israelites have in the world today, for they believe God will keep all His promises to the Israelites, including punishing all who persecute them.

A Disagreement Among Brothers

So it is good to remember that the pre-, post-, and mid-Tribulationists are all premillennial, with all the good qualities and areas of agreement that we have just surveyed.

Such post-Tribulationists as Robert Gundry and George Ladd fit into the above category, and I have found as I have studied their books through the years that they were careful scholars. Others who believe this view, such as Pat Robertson, Walter Martin, Jim McKeever, etc., have served the Lord well.

The same is true of the mid-Tribulationists like Norman B. Harrison and J. Sidlow Baxter who are also scholars. This view has received new interest through Mary Stewart Relfe's popular book, *When Your Money Fails*. I enjoyed reading her book, with the exception of a few uncharitably critical generalizations she made about those who disagree with her.

And among the pre-Tribulation exponents, I've never found greater scholarship than that expressed by J. Dwight Pentecost, John F. Wolvoord, and Charles C. Ryrie. The books of these men have dominated the scholarly side of prophetic study for decades, and they are virtually the standard in this field for our times.

I have found that almost all men who consistently proclaim a prophetic message in evangelism are pre-Tribulationists. My spiritual father, Col. Robert B. Thieme, Jr., a man who is still the best Bible teacher I have ever heard, is in this camp.

From Bouquets to Battle

You're probably saying by now, "If all these things are true, why is there disagreement about the time of the Rapture's occurrence?" My opinion is this: Good men disagree because God deliberately made this issue difficult to settle. Only the most diligent study and comprehensive knowledge of the whole realm of Biblical prophecy can begin to answer it.

As an example, Dr. Gundry repeatedly says that pre-Tribulationism is based largely on arguments from inference and silence.[1] This is in some measure true. But

[1]Robert H. Gundry, *The Church and the Tribulation* (Grand Rapids: Zondervan Pub. Co., 1973).

here is the big point: *All* of the views have to be developed to some degree on arguments from inference and silence.

The truth of the matter is that neither a post-, mid-, or pre-Tribulationist can point to any single verse that clearly says the Rapture will occur before, in the middle of, or after the Tribulation.

Can Anyone Offer a Sure Hope?

You may be saying, "Wow, if it's all that complicated, why bother?" I believe the first answer to that question is, "Because the Lord commanded us to seek to understand His prophetic Word." This is especially true in these last days.

Second, I believe that by comparing correlating prophecies on this issue, and by consistently adhering to the tried and proven literal method of interpretation, a sure answer to the Rapture question can be found. The most important element in this process, of course, is to consciously depend on the Holy Spirit for His guidance and illumination.

Third, as I said before, whatever the answer to the Rapture question is, *we will most likely live to experience it.* So how preeminently important the answer is for planning our lives for Jesus in this day and time!

Why Me, Lord?

There is no question in my mind that the Lord unmistakably led me to write this book. But I confess that many times I asked, "Why me, Lord?" After all, many scholars have written on and debated about this subject.

As I studied, however, I began to sense a reason. I believe the Lord has given me some fresh insight on the issue. I haven't studied as much or with such interest and excitement since my seminary days.

And one thing I will own up to, the Lord gave me the gift of "simplicity." Most scholarly works on this subject need an "interpreter." I'll never forget, as a young Christian, how chills went through me when I read the promise of God, "The entrance of Thy Words giveth light; it giveth understanding unto the simple." (Psalm 119:130) I chuckled in prayer to the Lord and said, "Well, Lord, I surely qualify for this promise, because I am simple. Will you please pour Your Word into me and give me light." You know, the Lord surely has been answering that prayer.

I prayed that same prayer again as I studied and wrote this book. The result has been wonderful. I've been blessed, reassured and given a confident and joyous hope.

May this book do the same for you.

THREE

PREDICTIONS AND PROMISES OF THE RAPTURE

I will never forget the first time that I heard about "the Rapture." It was from a young minister in Houston, Texas, named Jack Blackwell. I was so excited that I could hardly sleep for a week.

But it wasn't long thereafter before I ran into some people who called the idea of Jesus coming for the Church *before* the Tribulation "a false doctrine." They even brought a minister to straighten me out on "this dangerous teaching."

The result was a real blessing because this motivated me to search the Scriptures on the issue many hours a day. In fact this was one of my first lessons in systematic study of the Bible. In the process, the whole course of my life was changed. It was during those days that I realized that I would never be happy apart from studying and teaching the Bible. All other ambitions faded into boredom in comparison to this newfound love.

There were times during this search that I experienced the presence of the Holy Spirit in such power that I went into an ecstatic state. It was like lying in the ocean and feeling waves wash over me—only it was a physical experience of God's love moving over me.

During the course of these months I became completely convinced that the Lord Jesus would come for the true Christian *before* the Tribulation period. This conviction was not based only on what men taught me, but on a careful personal study of the Scripture.

Now, almost thirty years later, I've rechallenged all the reasons for that hope of the Lord's pre-Tribulation Rapture. As you read the following chapters, I pray that you will be motivated to also search the Scriptures, so that you'll know why you believe what you believe.

The most important place to start is with a careful examination of all the Biblical passages on the Rapture. They reveal that the Rapture has many unique factors.

THE RAPTURE IS A MYSTERY

In 1 Corinthians, Chapter 15, the apostle Paul, under the inspiration of God's Spirit, is teaching about the certainty of every believer's resurrection from the dead. He also reveals that the resurrection body will be wonderfully changed into an eternal immortal form that has real substance.

Paul clearly teaches that our new body will "bear the image of the heavenly," that is, like the Lord Jesus' resurrected body (Verse 49). In this regard, he says, "Flesh and blood cannot inherit the kingdom of God; nor does the perishable inherit the imperishable" (Verse 50).

In other words, our present body of flesh and blood, which must be sustained by elements of the earth which are perishable, must be changed to another form. This new form has material being, but it is of a kind that is suited for the spiritual, imperishable, eternal atmosphere of heaven.

The resurrected Lord Jesus is the measure of our future existence. He could appear and disappear at will (Luke 24:31; John 20:19). He could move through solid walls (John 20:19, 26). He could be seen and felt (Matthew 28:9; Luke 24:36–42). He could eat food, though it wasn't apparently necessary (Luke 24:41–43). Though glorified, Jesus could be recognized (Luke 24:30–31). Our resurrected bodies will no longer experience death, aging, crying, mourning, sorrow, or pain (Revelation 21:4).

The above are just a few of the wonders that we believers will experience in our future resurrected bodies. One thing, however, is necessary to be resurrected: We must first die! Resurrection is only for the dead. Resurrection from the *dead* was certainly a hope clearly taught in the Old Testament.

An Ancient Lesson in Hope

The earliest account of the resurrection hope in the Old Testament is recorded in the book of Job. Job actually lived before Abraham and Moses. Job took up the age-old question of resurrection when he said, "If a man dies, will he live again? All the days of my struggle I will wait [patiently trust], *until my change comes.*" (italics mine) (Job 14:14) Job responds to his own question by saying he would patiently trust until his change into a new resurrected body came.

Job states an incredible faith in his own resurrection, considering the early period of Divine revelation in which he lived, "For I know that my redeemer lives, and that he shall stand at the latter days upon the earth; and though after my skin worms destroy this body, yet in my flesh shall I see God, whom I shall see for myself, and mine eyes shall behold, and not another; though my heart be consumed within me." (Job 19:25–27, KJV) This is particularly amazing because at the time this was declared, there was no known written revelation from God.

This proves, along with many other Old Testament verses that could be quoted, that resurrection was known and believed throughout man's history of redemption, which began soon after mankind's appearance upon this earth.

I Love a Mystery

In the midst of Paul's teaching on the resurrection he says, "Behold, I tell you a mystery; we shall not all sleep, but we shall all be changed." (1 Corinthians 15:51)

There are many important truths taught in this verse.

First, Paul says he is introducing a *mystery*. The moment Paul uses the word "mystery," it signals that he is going to reveal a new truth not known before. The word in the original Greek (*mysterion*), as used in the New Testament, means something not previously known, but now revealed to the true believer.

So what is it that is new? In this chapter he has summed up what was known in the Old Testament: that flesh and blood cannot enter God's presence; that we must first die, and then be raised in a new eternal form.

THE RAPTURE MEANS NO DEATH

The second truth in this verse, and the meaning of the mystery, is that we Christians are not all going **to die!** This was a totally new concept. No Old Testament believer dreamed that some future generation would enter eternity and God's presence without experiencing physical death. Death is an absolute prerequisite to entering immortality through resurrection.

There were two partial examples of the Rapture in the

cases of Enoch and Elijah. They were taken directly into heaven without experiencing physical death. But even Enoch and Elijah haven't yet received their immortal bodies. As for the Old Testament believer in general, no one dared to believe that there would be a future generation of believers who would be taken en masse to God's presence.

The truly electrifying fact is that many of you who are reading this will experience this mystery. You will never know what it is to die physically.

THE RAPTURE INCLUDES ALL

The third truth in this verse is that all believers at the time of the Rapture will escape physical death. It is not an accident, I'm sure, that God selected the Corinthians to be the recipients of this revelation. For of all the early churches the New Testament records, the Corinthian church was the most carnal.

Paul rebukes them for everything from fornication (6:15–20) to getting drunk at communion (11:20–22). Yet Paul says to them, *"We all will be changed."*

A famous Supreme Court decision defined the word "all" as follows: "All includes everyone, and excludes no one." That's a very apt definition for how many believers go at the Rapture. Some will regretfully be raptured while out of fellowship with God. This may result in a loss of rewards for service, but not participation in the Rapture. We base this on the same foundation upon which we base our salvation. It is "by grace through faith, and that not of ourselves, it is a gift of God." (See 1 Corinthians 3:10–15 and Ephesians 2:8–9.) There is no Scriptural basis for a partial Rapture. The Rapture *must* be based on the same principles as salvation.

THE RAPTURE IS A TRANSFORMATION

The fourth truth revealed in the mystery of the Rapture is that "all Christians *will be changed*." The Greek word (*allasso*) translated "be changed," literally means "to be transformed." All Christians will be transformed in body and nature into new bodies that are suited for the eternal, spiritual, incorruptible realm in which God dwells.

All the things Paul teaches in this chapter about the resurrection body are true of the Rapture except that they are bestowed apart from death.

The extent of this transformation is the greatest thing God could bestow upon us. He transforms us into the exact likeness of His glorified Son, the Lord Jesus Christ.

"For our citizenship is in heaven, from which also we eagerly wait for a Savior, the Lord Jesus Christ; who will transform the body of our humble state into conformity with the body of His glory, by the exertion of the power that He has even to subject all things to Himself." (Philippians 3:20-21)

THE RAPTURE IS INSTANTANEOUS

Paul says, "In a moment, in the twinkling of an eye, at the last trumpet; for the trumpet will sound, and the dead will be raised imperishable, and we shall be changed." (1 Corinthians 15:52). Someone said that the twinkling of an eye is about one-thousandth of a second. The Greek word is *atomos* from which we get the word atom. It means something that cannot be divided. In other words, the Rapture will occur so quickly and suddenly that the time frame in which it occurs cannot be humanly divided.

Just think of it . . . in the flash of a second every living believer on earth will be gone. Suddenly, without warming, only unbelievers will be populating planet earth.

I recently watched in awe as the space shuttle blasted off into space. Within a matter of a few minutes it was out of sight and traveling at more than six times the speed of sound. What will take place for each living believer at the Rapture surpasses this by all comparison.

In another crucial passage on the Rapture, God reveals to us what will occur while we are being instantaneously transformed into immortal bodies, "For this we say to you by the word of the Lord, that we who are alive, and remain until the coming of the Lord, shall not precede those who have fallen asleep. For the Lord Himself will descend from heaven with a shout, the voice of *the* archangel, and with the trumpet of God; and the dead in Christ shall rise first. Then we who are alive and remain shall be caught up together with them in the clouds to meet the Lord in the air, and thus we shall always be with the Lord. Therefore comfort one another with these words." (1 Thessalonians 4:15–18)

Will We See Our Loved Ones Again?

The apostle Paul wrote these words to reassure the Thessalonians who had believing loved ones who had died. They were afraid that their departed loved ones would be in some other part of God's plan. Therefore, they feared that those who were raptured would not see their dear ones again in eternity.

Paul's answer is as amazing as it is comforting. For he assures them that not only will we see again Christian loved ones who have died, but that they will receive their resurrection bodies a split second before we are transformed into immortality.

The key word is "we shall be caught up." This is the translation of the Greek verb *harpazo*. As I mentioned earlier, it literally means "to snatch out" or "to seize." When we put together the concept of "being caught up into the clouds to meet the Lord in the air" together with the idea of an instantaneous transformation, the result is spine-tingling.

We will suddenly one day just blast off into space. Faster than the eye of the unbeliever can perceive, every living believer on earth will disappear. The world will probably hear a great sonic boom from all our trans-formed immortal bodies cracking the sound barrier. But the rest will be a mystery.

THE RAPTURE IS A REUNION

As for us, one moment we will be going about our life here on earth; the next moment we will be hurtled into the presence of departed loved ones. And above all, we will have a face-to-face meeting with the One whose death in our place made it all happen.

Another very wonderful experience is predicted in 1 Thessalonians. The apostle Paul reveals that we will not only be reunited with all our Christian relatives and loved ones, but with all those persons who trusted in Jesus through our witness. He said of those Thessalo-nians to whom he had ministered, "For who is our hope or joy or crown of exultation? Is it not even you, in the presence of our Lord Jesus at His coming?" Paul says that these spiritual children of his will be "his crown of ex-ultation in the Lord's presence when He comes." From this it appears that each one of us will have grouped around us those we have helped to believe in Jesus.

I don't know about you, but that excites me out of my mind. It makes me want to redouble efforts to witness for the Lord Jesus. To see even one person standing there before our Savior in a glorified body because I was available for the Holy Spirit to work through, will be the most wonderful "crown" of all.

A Meeting in the Air

It is very important to note that "We will be caught up in the clouds to meet the Lord in the air." (1 Thessalonians 4:17) There is a major point of controversy between the pre-Tribulationists and the post-Tribulationists over what happens next.

The post-Tribulationist says that after meeting the Lord in the air we will immediately return with Him to the earth. They agree that all believers alive at the time will be instantly transformed into immortal bodies. But since this event, in their view, occurs in connection with the second coming, believers will meet the Lord in the air only to return immediately with Him to earth. In thoroughly examining this scenario, I find that it poses some unanswerable problems with other Scriptures that deal with events that immediately follow the second coming. All these problems will be pointed out later, but let's take up one here.

To the Father's House

Pre-Tribulationists believe that a very important personal promise of the Lord is fulfilled when we meet the Lord in the air. As Jesus taught the disciples at the Last Supper, He sought to comfort and reassure them concerning His imminent departure with this promise, "Let not your heart be troubled; believe in God, believe also in Me. In my Father's house are many dwelling places; if it were not so, I would have told you; for I go to prepare a place for you. And if I go and prepare a place for you, I will come again, and receive you to Myself; so that where I am, there you may be also." (John 14:1-3) Let us make several observations about this prophecy.

First, Jesus specifically makes this promise to believers in the Church. For His whole teaching at the Last Supper (which has been designated The Upper Room Discourse) emphasized the revolutionary new privileges that would come to each believer when He ascended to the Father and sent the Holy Spirit to take up permanent residence in them. It is these very privileges that make the age in which we live unique and vastly distinct from God's previous dealing with Old Testament believers in general and Israel in particular.

Second, Jesus gives a very specific location around which the whole prophecy revolves. Jesus said, "I am going to prepare a place for you," and that place is specifically "His Father's house." We know from passages like Psalm 110:1 that when Jesus left and ascended, He went to God the Father's presence and took a seat at His right hand.

Jesus continued and said that as certainly as He was going to the Father's house to prepare a place for us, that He would come again and take us to that place to be with Him.

Third, Jesus gives us the specific time that all the above will be fulfilled. It will be at the time He returns for the true Church, for He says, "I will come again, and receive you to Myself; that where I am [in the Father's house], there you may be also."

Now if Jesus is building a dwelling place for us in the Father's house, and if we are to go there **when** He comes for the Church, how could He be speaking of an event that occurs simultaneously with the Second Advent? For at that time Jesus is specifically and personally coming to the earth (see Zechariah 14:4–9).

If the post-Tribulationists are right, then Jesus is engaged in a futile building program. For when He comes to the earth in the second coming, He will rule out of the earthly Jerusalem for a thousand years. Since He says

He is going to come in order that we may be with Him **where he is**, we would have to be with Him here on earth. Do you see the problem? The dwelling places in the Father's house would be unused. And worse by far, Jesus would be guilty of telling us a lie. For as we have seen, He is coming for the purpose of taking us to the Father's house at that time.

Post-Tribulationist Robert Gundry doesn't keep this passage in context when he says, "Jesus does not promise that upon His return He will take believers to mansions in the Father's house. Instead, He promises, *'Where I am,'* there you may be also.' "[1] This makes Jesus' whole promise ridiculous. Why would He speak of preparing a place in the Father's house for us if He didn't mean that His return was to take us there? With all due respect, Gundry has violated a basic principle of interpretation here; i.e., to keep verses in context. The passage is clear to the simple folk. It takes real determination to find Gundry's interpretation in this passage.

Gundry goes on to make a truly novel allegorical interpretation of John 14:1-3, "In order to console the disciples concerning His going away, Jesus tells them that His leaving will work to their advantage. He is going to prepare for them *spiritual abodes within His own person.* Dwelling in these abiding places they will belong to God's household. This He will accomplish by going to the cross and then ascending to the Father. But He will return to receive the disciples into His immediate presence forever. Thus, the Rapture will not have the purpose of taking them to heaven. It rather follows from their being in Christ, in whom each believer already has an abode."[2]

[1] Robert Gundry, *The Church and the Tribulation* (Grand Rapids, Mich.: Zondervan Pub. House, 1973), p. 153.

[2] Ibid. p. 154.

This interpretation surprised me. Gundry usually tries to avoid the allegorical method of interpretation. I strongly disagree with him here because it takes a passage which gives every indication of being literal narrative and makes *part of it* allegorical.

Jesus was literally taking His physical presence away from the disciples. This is exactly why they were troubled. Jesus also literally went to take a seat at the Father's right hand. There is absolutely no indication in the context that the dwelling places He is preparing and His return to take us there are allegorical.

Later Jesus does promise that He will be with us spiritually through the indwelling Holy Spirit, and that we will experience a mystical union with Him personally. But the context is very clear that this is what is literally meant (see John 14:15–26; 16:7–25).

Once again let us remember some basic principles of interpretation. First, if the literal sense makes common sense, seek no other sense. Second, all things are intended to be taken literally unless the context clearly indicates otherwise.

PUT IT ALL TOGETHER

Let us briefly sum up what the Scriptures covered in this chapter have taught about the Rapture.

(1) The Rapture was unknown until it was revealed to the Church by the apostles, especially Paul.

(2) All believers living when the Rapture occurs will not experience physical death.

(3) The Rapture will occur suddenly, without specific warning, and will be instantaneous.

(4) In the Rapture, every living believer will be in-

stantly transformed from mortal to immortal bodies which are like Jesus' glorified body.

(5) Those raptured will be caught up in the air to meet the Lord and the resurrected church-age believers who have died.

(6) At that time, we will be taken into God the Father's presence to temporary dwelling places that the Lord Jesus is presently preparing.

The post-, mid-, and pre-Tribulationists would agree on all the points above except number 6 and part of number 3.

Academics aside, the really important issue is the wonder of it all! What a marvelous expectation exists for this generation! No wonder Paul taught after revealing the great hope of the Rapture, "Therefore, my beloved brethren, be steadfast, immovable, always abounding in the work of the Lord, knowing that your toil is not in vain in the Lord." (1 Corinthians 15:58)

We can be steadfast and immovable in the midst of a turbulent and increasingly dangerous world, because we know that it means the Lord's coming is drawing near. Prophecy of the Rapture shines ever brighter as darkness gathers about us.

FOUR

SOME DIVINE DISTINCTIONS

There is a method of interpretation that is absolutely essential for determining which view concerning the Rapture is correct. This method is called dispensationalism.

Dispensationalism (which is the Divine ordering of worldly affairs) not only helps answer the Rapture question, but helps harmonize many Scripture passages that on first observation seem to be contradictory.

Here are a few examples:

First, Jesus taught in the Sermon on the Mount, "Do not think that I came to abolish the Law and the Prophets, I did not come to abolish, but to fulfill. For truly I say to you, until heaven and earth pass away, not the smallest letter or stroke shall pass away from the Law, until all is accomplished." (Matthew 5:17–18)

But Paul said in Galatians, "Nevertheless knowing that a man is not justified by the works of the Law but through faith in Christ Jesus, even we [Jews] have believed in Christ Jesus, that we may be justified by faith in Christ, and not by the works of the Law; since by the works of the Law shall no flesh be justified." (Galatians 2:16)

Trying to reconcile those two statements as a new Christian was practically impossible. In fact it troubled me. It was obvious that something radical must have happened between the Sermon on the Mount and the ministry of the apostle Paul.

Second, later in Jesus' ministry, He made another statement that confused me, "These twelve Jesus sent out after instructing them, saying, 'Do not go in the way of the Gentiles, and do not enter *any* city of the Samaritans; but rather go to the lost sheep of the house of Israel.'" (Matthew 10:5–6) I couldn't imagine why God wouldn't allow the apostles to speak to the Gentiles and why He sent them only to preach to Israel.

Yet later in the same Gospel of Matthew, Jesus said, "Go therefore and make disciples of all the nations (Gentiles), baptizing them in the name of the Father and the Son and the Holy Spirit . . ." (Matthew 28:19).

Obviously, these two examples point out a distinguishable change in God's plan. For some reason, that was unfathomable to me as a baby Christian, God introduced some completely new revelation about how He and man were going to relate to each other. I could add many more examples like these if space permitted, but these should sufficiently illustrate the point.

What is an Age?

Another indication that there have been distinguishable changes in God's plan for man is revealed in the term *age* or *ages*. The following New Testament usages of the word reveal this clearly.

Jesus spoke of "*this age* and *the age to come*" (Matthew 12:32). He also spoke of "the end of this age." (Matthew 13:39, 40, 49; 24:3; Mark 13:30).

God revealed through the epistles many different *ages* in the history of His dealings with man. For instance, He speaks of *"ages past"* (note the plurals) in Romans 16:25, Colossians 1:26, and Titus 1:2. He speaks of *"the present evil age"* in Galatians 1:3. Again, He speaks of *"the ends of the ages"* in 1 Corinthians 10:11, and *"the consummation of the ages"* in Hebrews 9:26. In 1 Timothy 1:17, God is called the *"King of the ages."*

A very important element is added to the concept of successive ages in God's plan in Ephesians 3:9-11. It is a complex context, but the main point to this discussion is in Verse 9, *"and to bring to light what is the administration of the mystery which for ages* has been hidden in God, who created all things . . ."

Several observations should be made of this statement. First, the context indicates that the Church is a mystery which has been hidden in God from all ages past. Romans 16:25 indicates the same truth.

Second, Paul is now *"bringing to light"* the *administration* of this mystery in the present age. The word *age* as it is used here is defined as "a period of time in history or in the development of man." In the context this idea is connected with the term *administration* which is *oikonomia* in the original Greek. This term is translated "dispensation" in the King James Version. This is the word that gave the system of interpretation its name. The root meaning of *oikonomia* is "to manage a household."[1] It means "to arrange, order, plan and administrate a household."[2] As the word is used in this context where it is linked with the term age, it means that God has planned, ordered, arranged, and administered cer-

[1] F. W. Gingrich and Frederick Danker, *A Greek-English Lexicon of the New Testament* (Grand Rapids, Mich.: Zondervan Pub. Co., 1979), p. 559.

[2] Ibid.

tain purposes within the sphere of definable periods of history. The *two* terms together (i.e., administration and ages) define the world as a household that is being administered by God in growing stages of Divine revelation.

It is important to add that the closest English equivalent to the Greek word *oikonomia* is *economy*. Webster's Unabridged Dictionary shows *oikonomia* as the root of *economy* and defines it as "an art of managing a household; the management of the affairs of a group, community, or establishment with a view to insuring its maintenance or productiveness; God's plan or system for the governing of the world,"[3] so, it is in this last sense that I am using the term *economy* and its synonyms, *administration* and *dispensation*.

Third, Verses 10 and 11 reveal that "God is teaching the angels His manifold wisdom through the mystery, the body of Christ, and that it is in accordance with the purpose of the ages (literal), which is made possible through Jesus our Lord." The main point here is that the *ages* are declared to have a definite Divine purpose.

Taken literally, the Bible reveals that history from God's viewpoint has progressed through a number of ages in which there have been different revelations of God's will. For as we have seen, the Bible not only speaks of "this present *age*," but of "*ages* past and of *ages* future."

Inseparably linked with this is the revelation of God's arrangement, purpose and design within the ages via the term "administration" in the New American Standard Bible.

One of the most important verses concerning God's involvement with the ages is found in Hebrews 1:2, which literally says in the original, ". . . through whom

3Webster's Third New International Dictionary of the English Language Unabridged (Chicago: Encyclopedia Britannica, Inc., 1981).

also He *blueprinted* the ages." This unique declaration reveals that Jesus actually planned and designed the various stages into which man's history would flow before time and space were set into operation.

Explosive Emotion versus Reason

I realize that the subject of dispensationalism is an explosive one. A whole book could be written on this important matter which I am trying to summarize in one chapter. And on this point, I urge every serious Bible student to read Dr. Ryrie's excellent book, *Dispensationalism Today.*[4]

Whatever your theological viewpoint, you have to come to grips with the *two recurrent concepts*: the economies and the ages. Apart from these concepts, the Bible cannot be understood as a consistent and cohesive whole. The only other alternative is to allegorize large portions of Scripture, which were clearly intended to be taken as normal statements of fact, in order to keep the Bible from contradicting itself.

The theological system that most adheres to a consistent, literal, grammatical and historical interpretation of the Bible is dispensationalism.

WHAT IS DISPENSATIONALISM?

No better definition of dispensationalism can be found than that of Dr. Ryrie, "A concise definition of dispensation is this: a dispensation is a distinguishable economy in the outworking of God's purpose. If one were describing a dispensation he would include other things, such as the idea of distinctive revelation, testing, failure, and judgment. But we are seeking a definition, not a description.

[4]Charles C. Ryrie, *Dispensationalism Today* (Chicago: Moody Press, 1965).

"In using the word *economy* as the core of the definition, the emphasis is put on the Biblical meaning of the word itself (i.e., *oikonomia*). Economy also suggests the fact that certain features of different dispensations might be the same or similar. Differing political and economic economies are not completely different, yet they are distinguishably different. Communistic and capitalistic economies are basically different, and yet there are functions, features and items in these economies that are the same."[5]

Each one of the various dispensations or economies that are distinguishable in the Bible begins with a new revelation from God to man. The new revelation contains both responsibilities of how man is to relate to God, and promises which enable man to perform them.

There is then a period of testing in the new revelations. Each economy reveals human failure to both appropriate the blessings and to obey the revealed responsibilities.

Each economy ends with a distinct Divine Judgment upon man for his failure and then a new economy is introduced.

The German scholar, Erich Sauer, adds a very important observation about the succession of the various Biblical economies, "The Holy Scripture is plainly not a spiritual-divine-uniform 'block,' but a wonderful articulated historic-prophetic *organism*. It must be read organically, age-wise, according to the Divine ages.

"Thus a new period always begins only when *from the side of God* a change is introduced in the composition of the principles valid up to that time; that is when from the side of God three things occur:

"1. A continuance of certain ordinances valid until then;

"2. An annulment of other regulations until then valid;

"3. A fresh introduction of new principles not before valid.

"Thus with the introduction of the present period of salvation there *remains* the general moral principles ruling the realm of the earlier period (Romans 8:4; 13:8–10), even though in a completely new spirit; for the Law is a unity (James 2:10), and as such is wholly abolished."[6]

The main points that should be emphasized from Sauer's statement are that the Bible is an organic, cohesive progress of living revelation that cannot be mechanically put into a philosophical strait-jacket. But it falls into various Divinely initiated stages of history in which certain ordinances of past ages continue, certain regulations of the past are eradicated, and certain new principles are revealed and set up as the new governing force of living for God.

I wish to make it clear, however, that even though there are distinguishable economies, there has always been only one way of salvation presented by God for man. Man has always had to approach God and be forgiven and accepted by Him on the basis of faith alone. In other words, salvation always has been and always will be received by man on the basis of faith alone.

The way that a redeemed man is to live for God has changed in the various dispensations. But the way of salvation has not.

What are the Dispensations or Economies?—God's Time-Line

One of the best ways to explain further the principle of Biblical economies is to show what they are. Now it

[6]Erich Sauer, *The Dawn of World Redemption* (Grand Rapids, Mich.: Wm. B. Eerdmans Publishing Co., 1951), pp. 193–194.

really isn't of utmost importance exactly how many there are. Nor is it fatal to the validity of the system that the various economies are called different names by different people.

The important thing is that they be distinguished and recognized. Even the avowed enemies of dispensational interpretation have to make distinctions between the way God deals with mankind in the dispensation of the law, the Church and the coming Messianic kingdom.

The following list of Biblical economies is generally agreed upon by all dispensationalists. The chart at the end of this chapter will also aid greatly in seeing these things in perspective.

I. THE DISPENSATION OF FREEDOM OR INNOCENCE

God created Adam in a state of holiness which was compatible with His own character. But Adam had, as part of the image of God created in him, freedom of choice. It was through this attribute that the possibility of sin existed.

Some have said, "If God created man with the potential for sinning, then God is responsible for the failure." But what were the choices? God could have created man without freedom of choice and thus have had a robot. Man would not have been able to respond to God's love, nor could there have been fellowship. For one must be able to choose not to love in order to be able to love.

The only other possibility was for God to take a calculated risk and create a creature in His own image. That image gave man intellect by which he could understand God; emotion with which he could respond with feeling and passion; and volition or freedom of choice with which he could act upon his understanding and emotions. The other two facets of God's image in man are moral reason or conscience and everlasting existence of his immaterial being, called the soul.

God took the calculated risk and created man in His own image, as defined above, in order that man could respond to Him in true love and fellowship.

The Angelic Factor

There is one other factor that is somewhat shrouded in the mist of eternity past which has to do with why man was created and why history is organized the way that it is. The Bible reveals that the angels are vitally concerned with how man responds to God. We know that the highest being created was an archangel named Lucifer who through pride and a desire to be equal with God rebelled against God and led a revolt among the angelic creation (Ezekiel 28:11–17; Isaiah 14:12–15).

We know that Lucifer, who became known as Satan and the Devil, was instrumental in causing Adam and Eve to believe a lie about God's character, to reject the relationship they had with Him, to lose their unproven holiness, and to lose the most basic part of their being, called spiritual life. It was only through this spiritual nature that man could know God on a personal basis and understand Divine revelation (Genesis 3; John 3:1–18).

We know that all through the successive Biblical ages Satan and his angels (called demons) have relentlessly sought to prevent humans from understanding and accepting God's provision of forgiveness, and to neutralize and destroy those who do receive it (John 8:42–47; 2 Corinthians 4:3–4; Ephesians 6:10–18; 1 Peter 5:8).

We know that the angels who remained faithful to God rejoice over one fallen human being who comes to repentance and believes in God's salvation (Luke

15:7–10). We also know that the angels are learning about God's manifold wisdom by the way He is dealing with mankind through the Church (Ephesians 3:10–11). We also know that the angels stare intently at the way God's grace is being poured out upon the world through the Holy Spirit (1 Peter 1:12).

As I surmised in a much fuller way in my book, *Is Alive and Well on Planet Earth*,[7] man was created in large measure for the purpose of resolving the angelic conflict. Apparently, God allowed Lucifer and his rebel angels time to repent. But after a period of grace, God brought judgment against Satan and his angels and sentenced them to eternal separation from God under a perpetual punishment. At that point Satan must have called God unjust and unloving.

Although God was under no obligation to do so, He chose to demonstrate to His angels His perfect justice and unfathomable love by means of a vastly inferior creature called man. The crowning of grace is that God is going to elevate redeemed and glorified man not only to replace the *angels* who were banished with Satan, but He is going to make him ruler over the whole angelic realm (1 Corinthians 6:3).

How God Answered a Dilemma

When the first human parents fell, God instituted a plan of redemption that demonstrates to the whole universe the perfection of His character.

God demonstrates His justice in that even though He loved man, He did not compromise that justice by simply sweeping the rebellion of Adam and Eve under the rug. Instead, God demonstrated His wisdom by devising a way for a uniquely qualified substitute (Jesus) to

[7]Hal Lindsey, *Satan Is Alive and Well on Planet Earth* (New York: Bantam Books, 1972).

fully pay our debt to His violated law and thus provide a free pardon.

God demonstrated His perfect love by coming into the world, becoming a man, living a selfless and sinless life, so that He could qualify to take upon Himself the full measure of His own wrath against sin on behalf of every human being.

All of this was done in order that rebellious man might receive a full pardon and eternal life by simply believing that the Lord Jesus died in his place.

At the final judgment, this great act of salvation will silence all of God's accusers and cause all to bow and acknowledge that they deserve their punishment.

So in the first dispensation man was free to do anything he chose, except that he was to tend the garden and not eat from one specific tree that God put off limits.

When man failed, innocence and freedom from sin was lost. The immediate judgment was loss of the relationship with God, the loss of spiritual life. Nature was cursed so that it would be very difficult to provide a living. Man was cast from the paradise garden, woman was placed under man's authority and childbearing became much more difficult.

II. THE DISPENSATION OF CONSCIENCE OR SELF-DETERMINATION

At the end of the previous economy, even in the midst of judgment upon man's failure, God introduced the way of forgiveness. Adam and Eve experienced a basic change in their being. They were still physically alive; but as God had warned, they had died spiritually the moment they decided to reject God's one commandment.

There was an immediate experience of guilt which was

evidenced by their becoming uncomfortable with being naked. They immediately tried to cover their sense of guilt with the work of their own hands. This was the first act of religion, for religion is man's attempt to cover his sin by his own works.

God graciously showed man the only acceptable way to cover his sin. God killed an animal and from its skin made coverings for their guilt. This, in very simple form, taught man that the consequence of his sin was the death of an innocent substitute of God's choosing. And from the substitutionary sacrifice God provided a covering for the effect of their sin. All they could do was receive it and throw away their own religious handiwork. This was the Gospel in childlike simplicity.

In this economy man was to recognize his need of forgiveness as well as understand how he was to live for God by the witness of his conscience. Man had conscience from the beginning, but now there was a great need for daily moral choices. Conscience now became the principal way God governed over mankind during this dispensation.

Man was responsible to respond to God through the inner promptings of his conscience. But man soon discovered the age-old art of rationalization. He soon made black white, white black and everything some shade of gray.

Finally, God evaluated the world of that day as follows: "Then the Lord saw that the wickedness of man was great on the earth, and that every intent of the thoughts of his heart was only evil continually." (Genesis 6:5)

God destroyed all mankind with the exception of eight persons who walked with Him, and believed in His provision of forgiveness.

The judgment that distinctly ended this period was a

worldwide flood. Man had failed another period of testing.

III. THE DISPENSATION OF CIVIL GOVERNMENT

Noah was the patriarch of the world after the flood. The new revelation to govern this period included making the animals fearful of man. Man became an eater of meat as well as grains. A promise was given that there would be no more world floods. And man was given the ultimate authority for human government—capital punishment.

This ultimate authority endowed human government with all lesser authority necessary for governing the world. Human civil government became the Divine means of maintaining order. It also included the way of preserving and proclaiming the message of salvation and the way to walk with God.

Man's inability to govern properly became apparent early in this economy. Noah displayed moral weakness by getting stone drunk and improperly guiding his own family.

Instead of dispersing and subduing the earth as God had commanded, the people banded together in one place. Soon, the first world dictator arose (Nimrod, Genesis 10:8–12; 11:1–9) and then led all the inhabited earth into the first system of false religion. This new religion was based on astrology and the worship of the stars.

The people built a tower at Babel (which later became the site of Babylon). This tower was an observatory for studying the stars, and was a symbol of unity. It was totally devoted to astrology. More importantly, it was also the symbol of man's rejection of God and His truth.

Man used civil government as a unifying system to bring all people into a false religion and to stamp out the truth about God. Once again unregenerate man failed by taking the very vehicle that was to lead him to God and using it to blind himself to the truth.

God knew that any form of one world government made it too easy for Satan to slip in a dictator who could then lead all mankind away from the truth.

The judgment that ended this economy was the sudden confusion of languages. This forced man to scatter and form nations. Soon afterward the nations began to deliberately erase the knowledge of God from their memory.

A Special Note

In the history covered by the first three economies, issues are not as precisely distinguished in the Scripture as they are in the following economies. There just wasn't very much written about those early periods. Several thousand years of man's relationship with God is covered in the first eleven chapters of Genesis.

I want to carefully note that this is not the case with the following economies. The Scriptures from Genesis 12 to Acts 2 are specifically addressed to the special people created from one Divinely chosen man named Abraham. This portion of the Bible of course has *application* to all believers of all ages, but by strict *interpretation*, it was addressed specifically to the physical descendents of Abraham, Isaac and Jacob under two economies.

So the following dispensations that are noted are very clearly distinguishable. There is clear Scriptural differentiation of the principles that prevail in each one of the successive economies.

IV. THE DISPENSATION OF ISRAEL UNDER PROMISE

This economy is characterized by a *people* and a *promise*. The term *promise* comes from the unconditional covenants that God made with an Assyrian man named Abram whom God renamed Abraham.

God's *reason* for introducing this new economy is clear. All nations were deliberately pushing the knowledge of God and the way of salvation out of their minds. Romans 1:18–32 is certainly an applicable description of the course all nations took in that era.

So in order that the truth about God might be preserved upon earth, and the way of salvation for all mankind might not only be kept but developed, God elected to create a special nation through which all these things would be accomplished.

A Promise is a Promise

God created this nation with a series of *promises*. God bound Himself with an oath to keep each promise. The following is a catalogue of the promises, which are also called covenants:

(1) *The Promise of a Nation:* "I will make you a great nation . . ." (Genesis 12:2a)

(2) *The Promise of Preservation of Abraham and His Descendents:* "I will bless those who bless you, and the one who curses you I will curse . . ." (Genesis 12:3a)

(3) *The Promise of World Blessing Through Abraham's Seed:* "And in you all the families of the earth shall be blessed . . ." (Genesis 12:3b)

(4) *The Promises of a Specific Land:* Genesis 13:14–17; 15:18–21

These promises were confirmed to both Isaac (Genesis 26:2-4) and to Jacob (Genesis 28:13-14). Ryrie gives an excellent analysis of the general character of this economy, "The responsibility of the patriarchs was simply to believe and serve God, and God gave them every material and spiritual provision to encourage them to do this. The promised land was theirs and blessing was theirs as long as they remained in the land. But of course there was failure soon and often."[8]

The Scripture that specifically deals with this economy is Genesis 11:10–Exodus 18:27. Some have questioned whether there truly are two dispensations distinguishable in God's dealings with Israel, since the *promise* and the *law* were both given to the same people.

I believe the two dispensations are sharply distinguished in Galatians 3 in spite of the statement that the Mosaic law did not annul the promise that was previously given. The distinction between the dispensation of promise and the dispensation of law fits every principle of definition given in the early part of this chapter. Paul summarizes the failure of the people under the promise, "Why the law then? It was added because of transgressions . . ." (Galatians 3:19). The people failed to live by faith in the promises that God had given them so He placed them under specific laws. (For God's summary of Israel's failure to believe His promises see Numbers 14:11, 22, 23.)

V. THE DISPENSATION OF ISRAEL UNDER LAW

This economy began with dramatic and frightening manifestations of God at Mount Sinai. God reviewed how He had graciously delivered them under the conditions of promise, "You yourselves have seen what I did

[8]Ryrie, op. cit. pp. 60-61.

to the Egyptians, and how I bore you on eagles' wings, and brought you to Myself." (Exodus 19:4)

Then God offered the Israelites the law, "Now then if you will indeed obey My voice and keep My covenant, then you shall be My own possession among all the peoples, for all the earth is Mine . . ." (Exodus 19:5). I believe, with many other theologians, that had the Israelites refused this offer of a law relationship, and instead asked to remain under the gracious economy of promise which depended upon God answering faith, that the Lord would not have forced the change.

But instead the people reacted with human pride and said, "*All* that the Lord has spoken we will do!" (Exodus 19:8). This confirmed the unbelieving heart which God saw and which caused the Lord to introduce the economy of law. The law was given to make man see how utterly incapable he is to live up to God's standards by human effort. This is revealed in the following verses:

"And the law came in (for the purpose) that the transgression might increase . . ." (Romans 5:20)

"Therefore did that which is good become a cause of death for me? May it never be! Rather it was sin, in order that it might be shown to be sin by effecting my death through that which is good, that through the commandment sin might become utterly sinful."
(Romans 7:13)

The law was given to make sin *increase*, not decrease, because man is inherently blind to the sinful nature with which he is born. The law provokes this nature into life so that it becomes very exposed. The more *we try* to keep God's law, the more the sinful nature rebels. So man has to admit that he is inherently so sinful that he must look by faith to the Messiah Jesus to save him, and to the Holy Spirit to enable him to live pleasingly for God.

God spoke to Moses about Israel's chances of living successfully under the law at the beginning, "Oh that they (the Israelites) had such a heart in them, that they would fear Me, and keep all My commandments always, that it might be well with them and with their sons forever!" (Deuteronomy 5:29)

It is obvious that the law was not God's preferred way to deal with man, but rather was a necessary historical lesson in the development of man's understanding of his total helplessness to establish a relationship with God by his own efforts.

God clearly anticipated Israel's failure under law when He predicted, through Jeremiah in the 7th Century B.C., "Behold, days are coming,' declares the Lord, 'when I will make a new covenant with the house of Israel and with the house of Judah, not like the covenant which I made with their fathers in the day I took them by the hand to bring them out of the land of Egypt, My covenant which they broke, although I was a husband to them' declares the Lord." In the rest of the statement, the Lord says that He will bring in three uniquely new factors: (1) "I will put My laws within them, and on their heart I will write it." (2) "All shall know Me, from the least of them to the greatest of them." (3) "I will forgive their iniquity, and their sin I will remember no more." (Jeremiah 31:31–34)

Israel's utter failure to live under law is meant to be an historical lesson for all mankind. The law was never meant to be a way of salvation, but rather to show us how good we would have to be if we were going to help God save us. This is clearly stated in Romans 9:30–10:4. Once again, the only way of salvation in every dispensation has been by faith in God's provision.

The interruption of this dispensation was predicted by the Lord Jesus, "O Jerusalem, Jerusalem, who kills the prophets and stones those who are sent to her! How often I wanted to gather your children together, the way a hen gathers her chicks under her wings, and you were unwilling. Behold, your house is being left to you desolate! For I say to you, from now on you shall not see Me until you say, *'Blessed is He who comes in the name of the Lord.'"* (Matthew 23:39) This economy was in focus from Exodus 19 to Acts 1:26.

The rejection of the often promised and long awaited Messiah caused God to set Israel aside and to *temporarily suspend* this economy. I say *temporarily suspend* because according to the previously mentioned prophecy of Daniel 9:24-27, Israel still has allotted to her seven years to complete the six Divinely given responsibilities named in Daniel 9:24. These are to be fulfilled under the same conditions that prevailed in the dispensation in which the first 483 years were acted out (or 69 weeks of years), namely the law of Moses.

This seven-year period, called the Tribulation by theologians, is actually the completion of the economy of law.

VI. THE DISPENSATION OF GRACE

This dispensation was actually a mystery in the ages of the Old Testament. It had to be, or there simply could not have been a bona fide offer of the promised Messianic kingdom to the Israelites.

One dispensational teacher calls this economy "the great parenthesis." Not because it is an afterthought of God, but because it was of necessity a Divinely-kept secret (Ephesians 3:9). No Israelite would have taken Jesus' offer of an imminent kingdom seriously if an alternate plan had already been revealed and understood in the Old Testament. This would have already concluded their failure.

A Clear Distinction

Of all the various dispensations, the most clearly revealed differences are between the economy of law and of grace.

One of the most important features of the new *modus operandi for living under grace* is the personal ministry of the Holy Spirit in and to every believer in Jesus Christ.

Since the fall of man, all the redeemed have experienced a spiritual birth when they believed. But the new ministries listed below are absolutely unique to the economy of grace. They all happen once for all at the moment of salvation.

There is the *baptism* of the Holy Spirit which joins each believer into a living union with Christ. This union is the most basic and essential meaning of the Church. The Church is the body of Christ composed of all believers. And we can only enter that body through the baptism of the Spirit (1 Corinthians 12:12–14). This first occurred in Acts 2 according to Peter in Acts 11:15–18.

There is also the *indwelling* of the Holy Spirit. The Spirit takes up permanent residence in each believer at the moment of salvation (John 14:16, 17; 1 Corinthians 6:19–20; Romans 8:11).

There is also the *sealing* of the Holy Spirit. The *presence* of the Spirit in the believer is God's *seal* or *guarantee* that we are His purchased possession and that He will certainly bring us into a glorified eternal state in His presence (Ephesians 1:13, 14; 4:30; 2 Corinthians 1:22).

There are also *gifts* of the Holy Spirit. Each believer receives at least one or more spiritual abilities (gifts) with which to accomplish God's will for his life (1 Peter 4:10–11; 1 Corinthians 12:1–33). The gifts are permanent (Romans 11:29).

Of these new ministries of the Spirit, only one is not received once and for all at the time of salvation. It is called the *filling* of the Spirit. It is a moment-by-moment ministry which must be continually appropriated by a submissive will and an aggressive faith. This is that ministry which enables the believer to effectively live for and serve God (Romans 8:1-4; Galatians 3:1-5; 5:16-18; Ephesians 5:18).

It is these new ministries of the Spirit that made it possible to remove the law principle and establish the grace principle. All of this was not possible until Jesus the Messiah completed His redemptive work at the cross. Because He satisfied all of the demands of the law against us and then paid its ultimate penalty of death in our place, God can now remove us completely from under the law's demands. The Holy Spirit under grace now works the righteousness of the law through the trusting believer (Romans 8:4).

In the economy of grace God no longer is working in a special way only with Israel. But now all nations, Jew and Gentile, are joined into a unique heavenly people called the Church. In the Church there is no national, racial or sexual distinction. All are one in Christ.

The Apostate Church

Even with such a heaven-high privilege the Bible predicts that the Church will fail, and all but a believing remnant will fall away from the faith (1 Timothy 4:1-4). Organized Christendom will have an outward facade of godliness, but will deny its power (2 Timothy 3:1-10).

Peter predicts that false teachers, masquerading as ministers of Christ, will infiltrate and take over the institutional church and teach destructive heresies. They will malign and nullify the truth which is the Bible (2 Peter 2:1-2). They will especially deny the prophetic Scripture and its claim of the Lord's return (2 Peter 3:1-7). Not to digress too much, I can testify that these prophecies have been fulfilled before my eyes and in my hearing.

How the Church Ends

This dispensation began in a unique way, and it will end in a unique way. It began with the advent of the Holy Spirit. It will end with evacuation. The Lord Himself will evacuate the Church so that the final seven years allotted to Israel under the law in Daniel's prophecy can be fulfilled.

Much more will be said in the next chapter about this very important aspect of prophecy. But it is very important to stress again that since the Church in the economy of grace was necessarily a mystery, hidden in God, from all economies past, it must be completely removed before God can finish dealing with Israel as a distinct program.

And since the focus of God is once again upon the Jew as a Jew in the seven final years of dealing with Israel (called "the Tribulation" or "the time of Jacob's trouble" in Jeremiah 30:7), the Church cannot be present. Otherwise the conditions that prevail during the time of the Church (i.e., there is no difference between a Gentile and a Jew) would make such an arrangement impossible.

VII. THE DISPENSATION OF THE MILLENNIUM

The second coming of Christ to the earth ends "the time of Jacob's distress" and ushers in the Millennial Kingdom promised to Abraham, Isaac and Jacob's descendents.

There will be an outpouring of the Holy Spirit upon all believers. Only believers will enter this kingdom. Satan will be bound for a thousand years. Jesus the Messiah will rule over the whole earth and set the atmosphere of the world system with righteousness. With all these blessings man will be expected to live out the standards of the King Messiah as described in the Sermon on the Mount of Matthew 5–7.

The curse of nature will be removed and man will have a perfect environment once more (Isaiah 11; 65:17–25; Amos 9:8–15; Micah 4:1–8; Zechariah 14:16–21).

But even with this kind of privilege some of the children of those who start the kingdom will not believe in the Lord Jesus as Savior. Evidence of unbelieving offspring shows up early in the Millennium (Zechariah 14:17–19, and so on). So at the end, God will release Satan to bring out into the open the rebellion that He sees in their hearts. Satan will quickly raise up an army of unbelievers. But God will judge them quickly and directly (Revelation 20:7–10).

At this point, time ends. All mortal believers will be translated into immortality. All unbelievers from all economies will be raised to stand before the Great White Throne for eternal condemnation.

A clear philosophy of history from God's viewpoint emerges out of these economies. Man is tested under all kinds of conditions throughout the dispensations. The first dispensation begins with a perfect environment and the last one ends with a perfect environment. Man fails in all environments, which demonstrates that environment is *not* the problem. (Thus God's viewpoint is totally the antithesis of communism, modern psychology and many other human philosophies.)

The dispensations show that the only answer is to be born again by faith so that man is changed from within. Then he masters the environment about him by God's enablement through faith.

SUMMING UP

Without an understanding and recognition of these various economies it is virtually impossible to interpret and harmonize the various stages of progressive revelation, and the distinguishable responsibilities under which man has been tested before God.

In the next chapter I will discuss more specifically how the differences between the dispensation of the Law and the dispensation of the Church bear upon the Rapture debate.

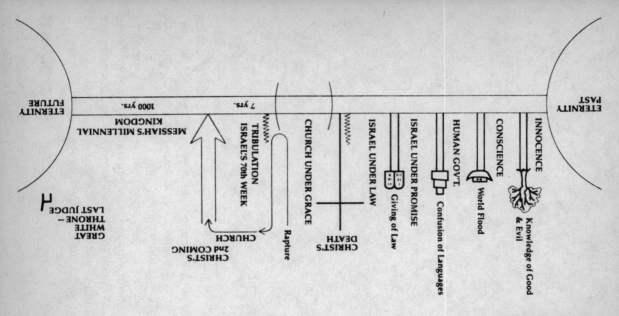

GOD'S OUTLINE OF HISTORY
OR DISPENSATIONS

ETERNITY PAST

INNOCENCE
Knowledge of Good & Evil

CONSCIENCE
World Flood

HUMAN GOV'T.
Confusion of Languages

ISRAEL UNDER PROMISE
Giving of Law

ISRAEL UNDER LAW
CHRIST'S DEATH

CHURCH UNDER GRACE
Rapture
CHURCH
CHRIST'S 2nd COMING

7 yrs.
TRIBULATION
ISRAEL'S 70th WEEK

1000 yrs.
MESSIAH'S MILLENNIAL KINGDOM

ETERNITY FUTURE

GREAT WHITE THRONE — LAST JUDGE

FIVE

THE GREAT HISTORICAL PARENTHESIS

One of the central questions in settling just when the Rapture occurs is whether Israel and the Church are truly distinctive and separate works of God.

In fact, Walvoord points out this critical issue when he says, "It is not too much to say that the rapture question is determined more by ecclesiology than by eschatology."[1] To translate this, it means that the doctrines concerning the Church bear more on the Rapture question than the doctrines of prophecy.

Ryrie expresses a similar conviction, "Actually the question boils down to whether or not the Church is a distinct entity in the program of God. Those who emphasize the distinctiveness of the Church will be pre-Tribulationists, and those who deemphasize it will usually be post-Tribulationists."[2]

[1]John F. Walvoord, *The Rapture Question* (Findlay, Ohio: Dunham Pub. Co., 1956), p. 16.

[2]Charles C. Ryrie, *What You Should Know About The Rapture* (Chicago: Moody Press, 1981), p. 62.

I believe with these men that the question of just when the Rapture occurs in relation to the Tribulation depends to a large degree on how unique and distinct God's program for the Church is from His program for the nation of Israel.

In fact, I believe that God's purpose for Israel and His purpose for the Church are so distinct and mutually exclusive that they cannot both be on earth at the same time during the seven-year Tribulation.

If this is so, then the Church must be removed before God can deal specifically again with Israel as defined in Daniel's prophecy (Daniel 9:24-27), because today there is no such thing as a Jew remaining a Jew in the Old Testament sense after believing in Jesus as Messiah. The apostle Paul makes this very clear when he says of the believer today, "For there is no distinction between Jew and Greek; for the same Lord is Lord of all, abounding in riches for all who call upon Him." (Romans 10:12) And again Paul says, "For *all* of you who were baptized into Christ have clothed yourselves with Christ. There is neither Jew nor Greek, there is neither slave nor free man, there is neither male nor female; for you are all one in Christ [Messiah] Jesus." (Galatians 3:27-28)

From the call of Abraham until the birth of the Church, God divided the human race into two categories: Jews and Gentiles. From the birth of the Church until today, God has three categories: nonbelieving Jews, nonbelieving Gentiles and the Church. This is clear throughout the New Testament epistles which were expressly written to the Church. But the following verse makes this concisely clear, "Give no offense either to Jews or to Greeks or to the church of God . . ." (1 Corinthians 10:32).

In this present economy of God's dealing with man, there are unbelieving Jews, and there are unbelieving

Gentiles. But the believer from either category becomes known as "the church of God" at the moment of salvation.

The Scriptures from both the Old and the New Testament that apply to the Tribulation period deal with the believing Jew as a Jew and the believing Gentile as a Gentile. Even the great judgments the Messiah executes upon the survivors at the end of the Tribulation are segregated. The Gentile is judged in Matthew 25:31–46, and the Jew in Ezekiel 20:34–44. The conditions are the same as they were in the economy of Israel under law.

WHAT IS THE CHURCH?

It is very difficult to discuss the Church today because the mere mention of the word conjures up all kinds of erroneous definitions as well as various emotions.

To most the Church is the building where the Christians meet. To others it is the organizations that make up the various denominations.

I'll never forget my first lesson on the Church that I heard as a young believer. An elderly lady sitting in a Bible class I was attending in Houston interrupted the teacher and said, "Pastor, there are young people in here desecrating the church sanctuary by chewing gum." The pastor, Robert Theime, who has a knack for shocking statements, fired back, "Lady, the sanctuaries are chewing the gum."

That's probably the best lesson I've ever received on ecclesiology, because I still remember it over twenty-five years later. The thrust of the statement, though humorous, is profound. For the Church is not a building nor an organization. It is first and foremost a living organism called the body of Christ (Ephesians 1:22–23; Colossians

1:24). This body is made up of every true believer, Jew or Gentile, mystically joined in a living union with Jesus Christ Himself and with each other (1 Corinthians 12:12-28; Galatians 3:27-28).

The average professing Christian today has no understanding of this truth, and yet it is the central teaching of the New Testament. I believe that this confusion is caused by ministers who act as if the goal of the ministry is to acquire real estate and build buildings which they erroneously call churches. Sometimes in the process they drive people away from the Gospel with high-pressure fundraising programs to pay for these often unnecessarily large and palatial edifices.

Paul addressed churches that met in houses, but he never called the houses churches. (See Romans 16:5 and Philemon 2 for example.)

This concept of the Church being the body of Christ is not just an illustration, but an actual organic reality. This is made wonderfully clear in an extreme case with which Paul had to deal in Corinth.

Some of the Corinthian believers had obviously got out of fellowship (not out of relationship) with God and slipped back into their old religious ways. I have stood among the ruins of ancient Corinth and looked up the mountain to the ancient temple of Aphrodite, the goddess of love, that dominates the skyline of the old city. Part of their old worship at that temple involved having intercourse with the temple priestess-prostitutes.

It is extremely important to observe carefully how God deals with this problem among these true believers who were walking according to the flesh at this point. Listen to what God said,

"Do you not know that your bodies are members of Christ? Shall I then take away the members of Christ and make them members of a harlot? May it never be!

"Or do you not know that the one who joins himself to a harlot is one body with her? For He says, 'The two will become one flesh.'

"But the one who joins himself to the Lord is one spirit with Him.

"Flee immorality. Every other sin that a man commits is outside the body, but the immoral man sins against his own body.

"Or do you not know that your body is a temple of the Holy Spirit who is in you, whom you have from God, and that you are not your own?

"For you have been bought with a price: therefore glorify God in your body." (1 Corinthians 6:15-20)

In the first place note that God doesn't question their salvation, but rather affirms that they are members of Christ's body.

Second, note that the whole basis of God's command for them to stop immediately their immoral behavior is: (1) "Do you not know that your bodies are members of Christ?" (2) "Do you not know that your body is a temple of the Holy Spirit who is in you, whom you have from God, and that you are not your own?"

Third, and most important, God says that when they have sexual relations with a prostitute, they are actually making the members of Christ to be members of a prostitute (1 Corinthians 6:15-16). There is only one possible way to understand the above statement. It is saying that the Christians are, in the first place, actually joined into an organic union with Christ, so that Christ is involved in whatever our bodies do (see Ephesians 5:30, KJV).

In the second place, it is saying that whenever we have sexual relations with someone, we become one flesh with that person, thus we join Christ to them. So-bering thought, isn't it?

A Very Special Word

God inspired the New Testament writers to take a common Greek word, *ekklesia*, and refine it into a highly technical and special meaning.

In its Greek usage outside of the Bible, *ekklesia* simply meant "a called out assembly of people." It is used in this sense in the ancient Greek translation of the Hebrew Old Testament, called the Septuagint.

The Lord Jesus Christ was the first to use the term *ekklesia* in its new sense when He said, "And I also say to you that you are Peter, and upon this rock I will build my church; and the gates of Hades shall not overpower it." (Matthew 16:18)

Jesus chose a very special moment to unveil "His church." Up until this moment, the word *ekklesia* had never been used in this special sense. The occasion was Peter's public confession of Jesus as "the Messiah, the Son of the living God." Peter was the first of the disciples to do this. (In the original Greek it is clear that the foundation of the church is not Peter because the word "Peter" ([Petros, masculine]) does not agree with the word "rock" ([petra, neuter]) in gender as an antecedent must do.) It is this confession of faith in Jesus that enters a person into the one true Church, the body of Christ.

This was a private revelation to Jesus' disciples. It also was a prophecy because He said, *"I will build* my church . . ." The Church couldn't be built at this point because Israel had not made its final rejection of Jesus as Messiah, and the means of forming the Church was not yet given.

The *One* Who Builds the Church

Since The Church is the body of Christ, composed of a living union of all true Christians with Christ Himself, the Church could not begin to be built until the arrival of the One who had the power to effect this miraculous union. The Bible calls that person the Holy Spirit.

Jesus predicted the coming of the Holy Spirit to inaugurate His new ministries for this dispensation, "I will ask the Father, and He will give you another Helper, that He may be with you forever; that is the Spirit of truth, whom the world cannot receive, because it does not behold Him or know Him, *but* you know Him because He abides with you, *and will be in you* . . . In that day you shall know that I am in My Father, and *you in Me, and I in you.*" (John 14:16, 17, 20)

The final seven sublime words that I have emphasized describe the essence of what the true Church is in its universal sense. *"You in Me"* describes the union of each believer with Christ Himself. Paul later described it, "For we are members of His body, of His flesh and of His bones . . . This is a great mystery, but I speak concerning Christ and the church." (Ephesians 5:30, 32, NKJV)

"And I in you" describes the permanent residence which Christ takes inside the believer at the moment of salvation. Paul later said, ". . . *that is,* the mystery which has been hidden from *past* ages and generations; but has now been manifested to His saints, to whom God willed to make known what is the riches of the glory of this mystery among the Gentiles, which is *Christ in you,* the hope of glory." (Colossians 1:26, 27)

The mystery of our union with Christ and His dwelling in us are the foundation of the true Church. For this reason, they could not have been revealed before it was obvious that Israel had rejected the Messianic claims of Jesus.

The Holy Spirit's ministry which miraculously forms the Church is defined as follows: "For even as the *body* is one *yet* has many members, and all the members of the body, though they are many, are one body, so also is

Christ." [This beautifully describes the Church universal.] "For by *one spirit* we were all *baptized* into *one body*, whether Jews or Greeks, whether slaves or free, and we were all made to drink of one Spirit." (1 Corinthians 12:12, 13)

It is the *baptism of the Holy Spirit* that forms the Church. This is not water baptism. It is the Spirit of God taking each believer at salvation and immersing him into a living, inseparable union with Christ (Galatians 3:27, 28; Colossians 2:12).

So the Church couldn't begin until the baptism of the Holy Spirit began. John the Baptist predicted that Jesus would instigate this baptism of the Spirit (Matthew 3:11). Jesus predicted that it would begin not many days from His ascension to the Father (Acts 1:5). The apostle Peter reveals that the baptism of the Spirit was first given to the Jewish believers on the day of Pentecost (Acts 11:15–16).

So the Church was born on the day of Pentecost when all of the new ministries of the Spirit that are unique to this dispensation were given.

The book of Acts reveals that God followed a specific order in initially giving the new Spirit ministries. They were first given to the Jewish believers since God previously had a covenant relationship with them (Acts 2).

Then the new ministries were initiated to the Samaritan believers who were part Jewish (Acts 8:14–17).

Next they were initially given to the non-Jews or Gentiles, who had no covenant claim to God at all (Acts 10:1–48 compared with 11:15–18).

After this transition period, the new ministries of the Spirit, for example, baptism, indwelling, sealing, gifting, and filling, were given to every believer *when* he believed. This is set forth in the epistles as the norm for every believer.

What we have been discussing is the Church *universal*.

But there are a number of other shades of meaning given to the term "church" in the New Testament.

The Local Church

The Church is often simply designated by its location. In this sense it refers to the professing believers who meet together regularly in a certain village or city. For example: ". . . the church in Jerusalem" (Acts 8:1); ". . . the church which is at Cenchrea" (Romans 16:1); ". . . the church of God which is at Corinth" (1 Corinthians 1:2).

A great many of these churches met in private homes. Twice the church that met in Prisca and Aquila's home is mentioned (Romans 16:5; 1 Corinthians 16:19). Others were mentioned as follows: "great . . . Nympha and the church that is in her house" (Colossians 4:15); "to Philemon . . . and to the church in your house" (Philemon 2).

Local churches were also described in the plural in terms of geographical regions in which they were founded. Here are a few examples: "And he [Paul] was traveling through Syria and Cilicia, strengthening the churches" (Acts 15:41); ". . . as I directed the churches of Galatia" (1 Corinthians 16:1); "the churches of Asia greet you" (1 Corinthians 16:9); ". . . the churches of Judea which were in Christ" (Galatians 1:22).

The previous references about the Church teach us the following truths:

First, though the Church assembled in various geographical locations, it is viewed as something distinct from both the building and the locale in which it met.

Second, these churches were simply designated by the name of the city, province or region in which they met.

Third, the local church was always considered to be part of the one true universal Church. For instance, it was "the Church of God which is at Corinth," and "the churches of Judea which are in Christ." Though these churches were resident in a specific location, they were viewed as belonging to God and each one directly united with Christ.

Fourth, the New Testament reveals that *not everyone* in the local church is part of the true Church universal, the body of Christ. The apostle John writes to the local churches concerning former members who have abandoned the faith,

> "They went out from us, but they were not really of us; for if they had been of us, they would have remained with us; but they went out, in order that it might be shown that they all are not of us." (1 John 2:19)

These are dreadful words which John says, ". . . in order that it might be shown that they *all are not of us.*"

The same apostle records the words of Jesus the Messiah to the seven churches of Revelation Chapters 2 and 3. In these letters, there are several exhortations to unbelieving individuals within those churches who are obviously not truly saved.

The clearest proof of this is the oft repeated promises to "the one who overcomes," Revelation 2 and 3. John defines this statement in his first epistle, "and who is the one who overcomes the world, but he who believes that Jesus is the Son of God . . . Whoever believes that Jesus is the Messiah is born of God . . ." (1 John 5:5 and 1a).

The Visible Church on Earth

The term "church" is also used in the New Testament to mean the totality of professing Christians without reference to locality. Used in this sense, the Church is practically equivalent to the term "Christendom." This usage embraces all the churches and individuals in them that profess to be Christian. It therefore includes true and false churches, believers and unbelievers (Romans 16:16; 1 Corinthians 15:9; Galatians 1:13, and so forth).

The Mystery of Being "in Christ"

One of the exclusive new designations given only to the believer in the economy of grace is a simple prepositional phrase that is repeated some 165 times in the epistles. This prepositional phrase is variously stated as "in Christ," "in Christ Jesus," "in Him," or "in God the Father and the Lord Jesus Christ."

These phrases describe the eternal, inseparable, personal union that each believer has with the Lord Jesus through the baptism of the Spirit. Virtually every benefit of salvation that the heavenly Father bestows upon the believer is transmitted through this union with Christ.

For example, we were given "every spiritual blessing in the heavenly places *in Christ.*" (Ephesians 1:3)

We were given the very "righteousness of God *in Him.*" (2 Corinthians 5:21) Since Jesus Christ is "the righteousness of God," when we are made one with Him, His righteousness becomes ours.

"In Him we have redemption through His blood, the forgiveness of our trespasses, according to the riches of His grace." (Ephesians 1:7)

Because of being in Christ, His death and resurrection are as much an actual fact for the believer as they are to Jesus Christ Himself. Sin and the law have no more claim on Christ because He has already died under the full penalty of the law. Just so, the same thing is true of the believer because of his total union of life with Christ (Romans 6:3–14). Just as sin has no claim on Christ's new resurrection life, so sin has no claim on the one who is in union with Him. Again, what is true of Christ is true of the believer *in* Him. This is so difficult to believe that only the Holy Spirit can make us understand and receive it.

The Lord says, "Even so *consider* yourselves to be dead to sin [the sin nature], but alive to God *in Christ Jesus.*" (Romans 6:11) If you want your life changed to a whole new sphere of victory, then begin to count as true what God says is true.

In the economy of grace, the Christian way of life is a matter of **becoming** what God **has already** made you in Christ. It simply depends upon learning what God says is true of us because of union with Christ, and then counting it true by faith. And remember, what God says is true about us *is* the most true thing there is about us.

Because of all that has been accomplished for us **in Christ,** God promises flatly, "For sin [the sinful nature] shall not be master over you, for you are not under law, but under grace." (Romans 6:14) In this new economy of grace, we are no longer under obligation to the law principle which could only demand but not enable. But we are under the principle of grace which doesn't demand, but gives new inner desires and enables (Philippians 2:13 and 4:13).

Now What?

You are probably saying, "What's all this got to do with the Rapture question?" Everything! All the unique and unparalleled ministries of the Holy Spirit to every believer make this economy absolutely distinct from all previous economies. These present ministries of the Holy Spirit also make this economy distinct from the conditions that are predicted for the seven-year Tribulation.

Robert Gundry and George Ladd seek to downplay this uniqueness in order to promote their case for a post-Tribulation Rapture.

Is the Church a Mystery?

In his effort to remove the distinction between the Church and Israel, Gundry first attacks the doctrine of the Church being a mystery, "Further, any argument for the exclusiveness (of the church) on such grounds runs up against the fact that the Church *as such* is never designated a mystery."[3]

Gundry's statement really begs the question. As discussed earlier in this chapter, Paul in the Ephesian letter said that the mystery is, ". . . that the Gentiles are fellow-heirs and fellow-members of the *body*, and fellow-partakers of the promise in Christ [the Messiah] Jesus through the Gospel." (Ephesians 3:6) All these mystery truths revolve around and are only possible because of the uniting of Jews and Gentiles into the body of Christ. Since the body of Christ is the Church and vice versa, anything that speaks of the most basic features of the body of Christ is speaking also of the Church. Therefore, the term mystery rightly applies to the Church.

But the real point is that the Church is a *new* program of God in which the Gentiles are made fellow heirs, united in one body with the Jews who believe in Jesus as Messiah. If this new program had been revealed and understood before the Messiah Jesus offered the Jews the promised kingdom and Himself as King-Messiah, it would not have been a bona fide offer. How could they have believed in an offer that assumed their unbelief and already had a known program to replace them?

Gundry levels three arguments against the pre-Tribulationist view of dispensational distinction between Israel and the Church. Gundry says that, "A partial revelation of the present age (that is, the dispensation of the Church under grace) in the Old Testament, a con-

[3]Robert H. Gundry, *The Church and the Tribulation* (Grand Rapids: Zondervan, 1973), p. 14.

nection (not necessarily identification) between Israel and the Church, and a dispensational change involving a transitional period open the door to the presence of the church during the tribulation."[4]

It is important to note at the outset that even if Gundry could prove these three allegations, it wouldn't necessarily put the Church in the Tribulation. But after carefully searching through each argument, I didn't find any evidence to prove that the Church *in its unique sense* as the body of Christ was anywhere revealed in the Old Testament. Only the Holy Spirit could interpret and apply the veiled Old Testament references to future salvation of Gentiles and make them understandable. The Israelite certainly didn't have any Old Testament revelation that would have made him comprehend this present economy of grace and the Church.

The fact remains that all Old Testament prophecies about Gentiles picture them in a subordinate role to the Jew in the Messianic kingdom. There is justification for the old rabbinic teaching of Jewish supremacy in the Millennial Kingdom,

> *"And strangers will stand and pasture your flocks, and foreigners* [Gentiles] *will be your farmers and your vinedressers. But you will be called the priests of the Lord; you will eat the wealth of nations, and in their riches you will boast."* (Isaiah 61:5, 6)

The Old Testament prophecies quoted in the New Testament and applied to the Church do not prove that the body of Christ with all its unprecedented privileges was revealed even partially in the Old Testament. It was a

[4]Gundry, ibid. p. 12.

"secret hidden in God." (Ephesians 3:9 and Romans 16:25–27)

The New Testament writers used the prophetic references to Gentiles to prove that Gentiles were always included in God's plan of salvation. The false teaching of first century Judaism, which said that Gentiles couldn't even be saved, had to be refuted by the Old Testament Scriptures which they claimed to accept. This false teaching was so tenacious that it even carried over to the early Jewish believers and the apostles (see Acts 10:34–35; 11:1–18).

This error persisted in the first Church Council of Acts 15:1–29. Some of the converts from Judaism insisted that Gentiles had to become Jewish Proselytes to be saved. The apostle James quotes Amos 9:11–12 only to show that Gentiles were always included in God's purposes.

In summary, the Old Testament references to Gentiles only have meaning when parts of these prophecies were selected by the omniscient Holy Spirit and applied to certain aspects of this economy's doctrine. But none of these Old Testament prophecies revealed anything about the body of Christ, the Church, before the Holy Spirit interpreted and applied them.

Dispensational Transitions

Gundry also contends that since there have been transitional periods in changing from one dispensation to another, there will necessarily be a transition period between the dispensation of grace and the Tribulation which, according to him, will put the Church into the Tribulation.

Even if this premise could be proven, it wouldn't follow that the Church would go all the way through the Tribulation to the very end.

There was a transition period during the change from

law to grace. It was necessary because the economy of grace introduced such radically new conditions. The change from law to grace as a principle of living, from God dealing almost exclusively with the Israelites to dealing with Gentiles on an equal basis, from a selective, conditional and limited ministry of the Holy Spirit to an unconditional permanent ministry to every believer, all required some time to inaugurate. God graciously gave time for the Jews not only to understand the above changes, but to overcome the false doctrines with which they had been indoctrinated. The epistle to the Hebrews, written sometime between A.D. 66 and 69, was God's final warning to them. In A.D. 70 Judaism was no longer an option, because the temple was destroyed by the Romans. With this destruction, animal sacrifice according to Mosaic law was rendered impossible. God left those who rejected His Messiah with no pretext to continue in a system of worship that had been made null and void by His once for all atonement.

But the change from the economy of grace back to Daniel's final predicted seven years of Tribulation does not need such a transition. The reason is that it is not the introduction of new conditions, but rather a return to old conditions previously known. The only hint of a transition is the prophetic signs that telegraph the approach of the era that precedes Christ's second advent.

The Close of the Parenthesis

Since this economy was not understood in the Old Testament times, and since there was only an expectation of a time of Tribulation and the coming of the Messiah to set up the promised Messianic kingdom, the interim economy of grace with its main feature of the Church, has to be removed even more suddenly and miraculously than it began. The Word of God certainly promises just that in the form of the mystery of the translation of living saints through the Rapture.

God's great parenthesis of history, that was hidden in God, will be closed in "the twinkling of an eye." The whole body of Christ on earth, composed of every living believer in Christ, will suddenly "be snatched out" of the earth to meet the Lord in the air. Without experiencing physical death, we will be instantly translated into immortality.

There, we will be joined by the rest of the body of Christ composed of all believers who have died from the day of Pentecost until that moment. There has never been such a family reunion as this one for which we are bound!

The Restrainer Must Go

More will be said about this later, but the removal of the Church is synonymous with the removal of "the Restrainer" of 2 Thessalonians 2:4–12.

As I will demonstrate later, the Restrainer of lawlessness who prevents the Roman Dictator called the Antichrist from being unveiled, can only be the Holy Spirit. Since the day of Pentecost, the Spirit of God has been resident in the world through the indwelling of the body of Christ which is composed of every believer.

Because of this special residence in the world the Holy Spirit has been restraining "the mystery of lawlessness" as well as the Antichrist, "the man of lawlessness." But when the body of Christ is removed, the Spirit of God in His present ministry is "taken out of the way" (2 Thessalonians 2:7).

In the first place, the Tribulation is characterized by the most rampant human lawlessness of all time. The present restraint of the Holy Spirit is obviously removed.

There is ample evidence that the Holy Spirit does minister according to the conditions of the previous economy of law during the Tribulation.

It is important to note that in the Old Testament the Holy Spirit did convince people of their need for salvation, give the new birth and work through certain chosen vessels such as prophets. The Scripture predicts that He will work in the same way during the Tribulation.

Second, one of the clear examples of the limited ministry of the Spirit during the Tribulation is the severe lack of spiritual perception on the part of the believers at the judgment that occurs just after the second advent of Christ (Matthew 25:31–40). Certainly a believer who is indwelt by and filled with the Holy Spirit would understand what Jesus meant when He says, "I was hungry, and you gave Me something to eat; I was thirsty, and you gave Me drink; I was a stranger, and you invited Me in; naked, and you clothed Me; I was in prison, and you came to visit Me."

A believer today in the dispensation of grace understands through the Spirit's teaching the verse that says, ". . . he who receives whomsoever I send receives Me." (John 13:20a) The Tribulation believer, however, doesn't manifest this rather simple spiritual insight.

I praise God for a man like John Darby who in the early nineteenth century through diligently studying the Scripture found that the Church of his day had completely overlooked the large body of revelation about the uniqueness of the Church as the body of Christ.

It was his study of this doctrine that led him to believe that the Church must have as unique an ending as its beginning. But more will be said about Darby later.

The next chapter will help define how the Church and the Tribulation relate to each other. It will also help establish God's chronology of the Tribulation—Daniel's Seventieth Week.

SIX

REVELATION'S CHRONOLOGY AND THE RAPTURE

Down through history, the book of Revelation has inspired more wonder, curiosity, bewilderment and sometimes even fear, than any other book of the Bible. It is unquestionably the most difficult to analyze and interpret.

But no other book gives us more clues as to how to find the meaning. There are certain keys given in the book itself that are of enormous help to us in interpreting it.

However difficult it may be, the book of Revelation is the most important factor in understanding the events of the seven cataclysmic years immediately preceding and leading to the second coming of the Lord Messiah Jesus. It is the only extended portion of Scripture that systematically deals with this topic. Chapters 4 through 19 deal exclusively with the Tribulation period. Revelation is the "Grand Central Station" of all the prophecies that deal with the Tribulation. It puts them all together into perspective.

WHY REVELATION IS RELEVANT TO RAPTURE

No other single book is more important to the issue of when the Rapture occurs. Revelation's chronological sequence establishes just when and upon whom "the wrath of God" falls. Both the mid-Tribulationist and post-Tribulationist must establish that "God's wrath" only falls at or near the very end of the Tribulation. They *all* admit that the Scripture does say that God's wrath will not be poured out upon the Church.

The following are some of the important keys to interpreting Revelation:

The first key is the use of Old Testament symbols. Most of the symbols used in Revelation are either explained somewhere else in the Bible, or, as we will see in the second key, they are explained in the context itself.

For example, the symbols used in Revelation 12:1 and 2 are explained in Joseph's dream of Genesis 37:9 and 10. Jacob, Joseph's father, interprets the dream as follows: the *sun* is Jacob; the *moon* is Rachel; the *eleven stars* are the sons of Jacob who fathered the tribes of Israel; the *twelfth star* is Joseph. So the symbols show that the "woman" of Revelation Chapter 12 is Israel, composed of the twelve tribes descended from Jacob's twelve sons.

The second key is that symbols are often explained by the immediate context. The great dragon and the serpent of Revelation 12 is identified in Revelation 12:9 as the Devil and/or Satan. Another example is the great harlot, called Babylon the Great, of Revelation 17:3-7, which is identified in 17:18. She is the great city that **is reigning** over the kings of the earth. When the apostle John wrote this, the great city reigning over the kings of the earth was **Rome.** So Rome is clearly labeled "mystery Babylon" by the prophetic symbol of Revelation. Parenthetically, the above use of symbols illustrates one of the reasons for the symbols in the time of Revelation's writing. Had the apostle openly labeled Rome as the center of all heresy and corruption, the Roman Emperor would have had him and all the Christians executed for treason.

The third key is John's testimony of how he actually **saw** and **heard** the things about which he writes in his prophecies.

At the beginning of the book, John records the vision given him by the Lord Jesus Christ,

"I was in the Spirit on the Lord's day, and I heard behind me a loud voice like the sound of a trumpet, saying, 'write in a book what you see, and send it to the seven churches . . .'" (Revelation 1:10–11a)

All of the way through the rest of the book the apostle continually testifies that he **saw** and **heard** the things about which he wrote. And then at the end of the book John bears his final solemn testimony about how he received the content about which he wrote, "And he said to me, 'These words are faithful and true'; and the Lord, the God of the spirits of the prophets, sent His angel to show to His bond-servants the things which must shortly take place . . . and I, John, am the one who *heard* and *saw* these things . . ." (Revelation 22:6, 8).

The key is this: John heard and saw things that would happen on earth some nineteen hundred years later. How in the world would a first century man describe the highly advanced scientific marvels of warfare at the end of the twentieth century? John had to use phenomena with which he was familiar to give visual and audible illustrations of what he was witnessing.

John was hurtled by God's Spirit through time up to the end of the twentieth century, shown the actual cataclysmic events of the Tribulation, then returned to the first century and told to write about what he had witnessed.

An example is the judgment of the second trumpet,

"And the second angel sounded, and **something like** *a great mountain burning with fire was thrown into the sea; and a third of the sea became blood; and a third of the creatures which were in the sea and had life, died; and a third of the ships were destroyed."* (Revelation 8:8–9)

I believe that the apostle was giving an accurate description of a thermonuclear naval battle in terms of his first century experience. Many more examples could be given of this key, but space doesn't permit. (My book on Revelation called *There's A New World Coming* gives a verse-by-verse analysis.)

The Divine Outline

The fourth key to interpreting Revelation is the outline that Jesus gave John at the time He commissioned him to write it. Actually, the Lord Jesus instructed the apostle exactly how he was to structure the book,

"Write therefore the things you **have seen,** *and the things which* **are,** *and the things which* **shall take place after these things."** (Revelation 1:19)

In checking commentaries on the book of Revelation written from some two centuries ago until the present, I found that the vast majority of writers recognized that Revelation 1:19 is intended to be the outline of the book. It is obvious to any interpreter who takes the book normally and believes it at face value. This is of considerable importance because most post-Tribulationists try to explain this outline away so that they can strengthen their case for the Church being in the Tribulation.

The Things Which You Have Seen

This covers Chapter 1 where John describes the risen Lord Jesus' appearance to him and the phenomena that occurred during that visitation. It is described with a past tense.

The Things Which Are

This describes Chapters 2 and 3. These chapters are described by a present tense of the verb for being (*eimi* in the Greek) which stresses the present state of things in history. I believe, along with many scholars, that these seven letters were not only written to seven literal churches with real problems, but also that they have a prophetic application to Church history.

Many factors convinced me of this interpretation. First, why were these seven churches selected? There were hundreds of other churches in Asia at this time. There were thousands of churches worldwide. So why just these particular seven?

Second, why were these seven churches arranged in this order?

Third, why were the conditions in the churches arranged in such a way that they describe discernible, successive epochs of Church history accurately?

Fourth, why place seven practical letters of instructions to churches in this book and in this position if they have no prophetic application?

I believe that these seven churches were selected and arranged by our omniscient Lord because they had problems and characteristics that would prophesy seven stages of history through which the Church universal would pass.

The Things Which Shall Take Place After These Things

This third division of the book's Divinely given outline is clearly intended to convey *future things* to the events covered by the first and second divisions. The future tense of the verb *ginomai* contrasts sharply with the present tense of the verb *eimi* used for the previous section. The idea is "what shall come to be after these things." This statement obviously describes things that will occur after the first two sections.

"These things" is the translation of the Greek words *meta tauta*. This phrase is first used in Chapter 1:19, and not used again until Chapter 4, Verse 1. It clearly indicates that there is a shift into future things under different conditions from those described in the first three chapters, and that this is the place where the outline begins in its futuristic phase.

That this is a shift to things future to the Church age described in Chapters 2 and 3 is apparent because of these factors:

First, as I just mentioned, Chapter 4, Verse 1, is the first place that *meta tauta* is used after it is given the special meaning in Chapter 1, Verse 19. Therefore, as the antecedent of that special meaning given in Chapter 1, Verse 19, it must be understood as the place where the outline shifts to things that are future to the first two parts of the outline.

Second, in Chapter 4, Verse 1, *meta tauta* is used twice. A voice from heaven leaves no doubt as to its meaning in the latter part of Verse 1, "Come up here, and I will show you *what must take place after these things.*"

Third, John is caught up to heaven to see things that are definitely *future* to our present experience.

Fourth, not one reference is made again concerning the Church on earth until after the second coming of the

Lord Jesus Christ. Since the Church is mentioned nineteen times in the first three chapters under the divine outline of "the things which are," and since the Church is not mentioned or implied as being on earth even once after the statement "Come up here, and I will show you what must take place *after these things,*" I conclude that it is the end of the Church age that is meant here, and that the Church is in heaven thereafter until it returns as the bride of Christ in Revelation 19:7-14.

An Amazing Similarity

The similarity of the terminology used in both 1 Thessalonians 4:16-17 and Revelation 4:1-2 supports the contention that the Church is taken to heaven here. Both passages speak of a trumpet sounding, of a shout of command, of being caught up to heaven, and of an instantaneous translation of the believer. I believe, along with many scholars, that the apostle John's experience here is meant to be a prophetic preview of what the living Church will experience in the Rapture.

Revelation's Order of Judgments

By far the most important aspect of interpreting Revelation is just how the seven **Seal** judgments, **Trumpet** judgments and **Bowl** judgments relate to each other.

If the judgments occur in consecutive order, then it tends to support the pre-Tribulation Rapture. The following chart illustrates the way I believe they occur.

If the judgments are concurrent, then it tends to support the mid- and post-Tribulation views. The chart below illustrates Gundry's view of the order of judgments.[1]

[1]Robert Gundry, *The Church and the Tribulation* (Grand Rapids, Zondervan Pub.: 1973), p. 75.

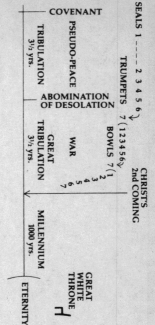

JUDGMENTS OF REVELATION CONSECUTIVE VIEW

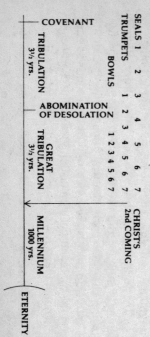

JUDGMENTS OF REVELATION CONCURRENT VIEW

Since the post-Tribulationists agree that the Church cannot suffer Divine wrath, they have to jam as many of the severe judgments as possible into the short time-frame of the actual second coming. If it can be demonstrated that Divine wrath falls on the earth prior to the second coming, then, their theory contradicts itself.

Gundry states, "Thus, God's wrath will not stretch throughout the whole Tribulation. Those passages in Revelation which speak of divine wrath deal, rather, with the close of the Tribulation." "Not until the final crisis at Armageddon, when Jesus descends (and the church is caught up if post-Tribulationism is correct), will God pour out His wrath upon the unregenerate."[3]

Whatever is the order of judgments, it has to fit into the *whole* pattern of Tribulation events predicted in the other prophetic passages of the Bible. I do not believe that the post-Tribulationists' scheme of Revelation's chronology can be harmonized with either the rest of the Biblical Tribulation prophecies or those of Revelation.

Let us first observe that all the judgments in the book of Revelation are presented as judgments of God on a Christ-rejecting world no matter who or what the agency of judgment may be.

The scroll of seven seals, which contains the judgment of the seals, is presented as so dreadful in Chapter 5 that no one in heaven or on earth is worthy to open them except the Lord Jesus, the Messiah Himself. So the authority and source for the unleashing of the seal judgments is the Lord. So how can anyone say that they are not God's wrath upon man?

The *first seal* unleashes the Antichrist to go forth and establish his control upon the earth. He will begin the seven years of Tribulation by signing a covenant guaranteeing Israel's security and the Middle East's peace (Daniel 9:27).

During this seal the Antichrist will apparently conquer through ingenious plans for world economic recovery and prosperity and world peace. In Daniel's prophetic description of this Roman Dictator, he says, "and by means of *peace* [he] shall destroy many . . ." (Daniel 9:25b KJV).

[2]Gundry, ibid. p. 77.

[3]Gundry, ibid. p. 48.

No one can read 2 Thessalonians, Chapter 2, Verses 9 through 12, and fail to see the clear connection between the Divinely permitted unveiling of the Antichrist, attended by Satanic miracles and a deluding influence from God, and the resulting condemnation of all on earth who reject God's truth. This passage clearly shows the Antichrist to be the chief vehicle of God's judgment on the world. The Antichrist himself is one of the greatest expressions of God's wrath, for he is the one who will slaughter believers and lead the whole world to destruction.

World Peace for Three and One-Half Years

There are several indications that the first half of the Tribulation will be a time of world pseudo-peace established by the Antichrist of Rome. In addition to the verse just quoted, Revelation records the progress of the Antichrist, " . . . and they worshipped the beast [Roman Antichrist], saying, 'Who is like the beast, and *who is able to wage war with him?'"* (Revelation 13:4). This verse reveals at least two profound insights into world conditions during the first half of the Tribulation.

First, the people will give absolute authority to the Antichrist because of fear of war and anarchy caused by economic catastrophe.

Second, the Antichrist will stop war so that the world will extol him because they believe that no one can make war against him.

Another very important clue is in Ezekiel's prophecy of Israel's condition just before the great northern power (the Soviet Union and allies) invades, "Thus says the Lord God, 'on that day when My people Israel are living *securely,* will you not know it? And you [the USSR] will come from your place out of the remote parts of the north [extreme north], you and many peoples with you, all of them riding horses, a great assembly and a mighty army." (Ezekiel 38:14–15)

For those who say God doesn't pour out his wrath (even on the unregenerate, as Gundry said) on the world till the very end, listen to God's response to this invasion: "It will come about on that day, when Gog [USSR] comes against the land of Israel,' declares the Lord God, 'that My *fury* will mount up in My *anger*. And in My zeal and in My *blazing wrath* I declare *that* on that day there will surely be a great earthquake in the land of Israel' . . . 'with pestilence and with blood I *shall* enter into judgment with him; and I shall rain on him, and on his troops, and on the many peoples who are with him a torrential rain of hailstones, fire, and brimstone. And I shall magnify Myself, sanctify Myself, and make Myself known in the sight of many nations; and they will know that I am the Lord.'" (Ezekiel 38:18, 19, 21–23)

Now when does all this happen? We know the following factors:

(1) Israel will be at peace under the Antichrist's protection (Daniel 9:27; Ezekiel 38:11, 14).

(2) Israel has reinstituted the sacrifices of the Mosaic law and rebuilt her temple (Daniel 9:27 cp. Matthew 24:15–20).

(3) The world is at peace (Revelation 13:4).

(4) **War** begins when the Pan Arabic army attacks Israel because of a dispute over Jerusalem (Zechariah 12:2–3), and then the Soviet Union with its allies (King of the North) immediately launch an overwhelming attack against the Middle East (Daniel 11:40–45).

(5) This war has to begin when "the abomination of desolation" predicted by Daniel in 9:27 is set up in the holy of holies of the Jerusalem temple

(Matthew 24:15). Jesus Christ is the one who says to the believing Jew of that day to flee the city to a prepared place of safety (Revelation 12:6, 13–17) because "there will be a *great tribulation*, such as has not occurred since the beginning of the world until now, nor ever shall. And unless those days had been cut short, *no life would be saved*." (Matthew 24:21–22)

We know absolutely that "the abomination of desolation" is set up in the middle of the seven-year Tribulation (Daniel 9:27). Therefore, the great *war* of Ezekiel 38 and 39 must begin in the middle of the Tribulation.

The *second seal* must, therefore, occur at the middle of the Tribulation. Because the second seal specifically "takes *peace* from the earth, and men begin to slay each other with a *great sword*." (Revelation 6:3, 4)

Therefore, the opening of the second seal must be the same as the great Russian invasion of Israel predicted in Ezekiel 38:8–16; Daniel 11:40–45 and Joel 2:20.

Parenthetically, the second seal also proves that the earth was in a period of pseudo-peace prior to its opening, because it "takes *peace* from the earth." You can't take away something that wasn't there.

Armageddon isn't One Battle, but a War

The battle plan given in Daniel 11:40–45 definitely reveals that the war that begins in the middle of the Tribulation escalates into a global conflict. Ezekiel 38 and 39 indicate the same thing.

Dr. Pentecost accurately states the issue, "It has been held commonly that the battle of Armageddon is an isolated event transpiring just prior to the second advent of Christ to the earth. The extent of this great movement in which God deals with 'the kings of the earth and of the whole world' (Revelation 16:4) will not be seen unless it is realized that the 'battle of that great day of God Almighty' (Revelation 16:14) is not an isolated battle, but rather a campaign that extends over the last half of the Tribulation period. The Greek word *polemos*, translated 'battle' in Revelation 16:14, signifies a war or campaign, while *mache* signifies a battle, and sometimes even single combat. This distinction is observed by Trench (*New Testament Synonyms*), and is followed by Thayer (*Greek-English Lexicon of the New Testament*) and Vincent (*Word Studies in the New Testament*). The use of the word *polemos* (campaign) in Revelation 16:14 would signify that the events that culminate in the gathering at Armageddon at the second advent are viewed by God as one connected campaign."[4]

Looking at war in terms of today's unbelievably destructive weapons, it is easy to understand the horrible carnage and devastation that is predicted in the prophecies about this period. These prophecies indicate something that is very important from a military perspective. The war that begins with the Pan Arab and Soviet invasion of the Middle East is portrayed as beginning with *conventional* weapons. It is only after the Soviet army is beginning to lose that the prophecies begin to intimate the use of nuclear weapons. And most important of all, the nuclear war escalates in stages until it becomes an all-out worldwide nuclear holocaust. This is the exact sort of military strategy that is being planned by the major powers today, that of a case-by-case escalation.

The seal, trumpet and bowl series of judgments in Revelation harmonize perfectly with this scenario if they are interpreted as unfolding successively. The judgments increase in frequency and severity with each new series. This is consistent with God's revealed character,

[4] J. Dwight Pentecost, *Things to Come* (Findlay, Ohio: Dunham Publishing Co., 1958), p. 340.

for He is slow to anger, not willing that any should perish. Therefore, the progressive increase in severity is consistent with the successive scenario of judgments in the Old Testament prophecy.

The Seventh Seal and Trumpet

The seventh seal and seventh trumpet give very important insight as to whether the seal and trumpet judgments occur successively or concurrently.

A close examination of the opening of the seventh seal reveals that it isn't the same kind of judgment as the previous six seals. There is an interlude of silence mingled with the prayers of the saints in heaven and a temporary restraint of judgment on earth. God gives the earth a chance to repent before the next series of judgments.

But the crucial thing to observe is that the seventh seal actually unleashes the next series of judgments which are the seven trumpets. Any normal reading of the following verses clearly reveals the idea of succession,

"And when He broke the seventh seal, there was silence in heaven for about half an hour. **And** *I saw the seven angels who stand before God; and seven* **trumpets** *were given to them."* (Revelation 8:1–2)

Likewise, the sounding of the seventh trumpet does not send forth a single specific judgment as the first six trumpets did. Instead there is another interlude in heaven and a lull in judgments upon earth. In heaven, God announces His claim of ownership over the earth and that His Messiah is about to begin His reign over it. Then there are more of the combined historical-prophetical cameos in Chapters 12 through 14.

We find that the next chronological movement of Tribulational events takes place in Chapter 15. Here we are introduced to the seven angels who have the seven **last plagues** which **finish** God's **wrath** (15:1).

From this, observe first that these seven bowl judgments are the direct result of the sounding of the seventh trumpet. This is true because these are the next and only judgments which occur after that trumpet is sounded.

Second, observe that it says the seven bowl judgments are the **last** ones. This indicates that they are the last in a series of previous judgments.

Third, observe that it says in these seven bowl judgments "the wrath of God is finished." (15:1) This indicates clearly that the wrath of God doesn't begin with these judgments, as Gundry and the post-Tribulationist crowd contend, but rather that they *finish it*. From this, it is evident that all the judgments of Revelation are considered God's wrath against man.

The bowl judgments occur in very rapid succession. In terms of magnitude and scope, they are unprecedented. Whereas the trumpet judgments, for instance, destroyed a third of life in the sea, the bowl judgment destroys **all** life in the sea (16:4).

I believe that a normal analysis of the structure of Revelation leads to the conclusion that the three series of judgments are consecutive to each other, and that the seventh judgment of the first two series simply introduces the next series. In other words, they are somewhat telescopic to each other as previously illustrated in my chart on page 106.

There is a strong Semitic style of writing in the book of Revelation. This is evidenced by the many historical-prophetic cameos that explain why certain things happened in history and culminate in the Tribulation.

These cameos are interspersed in the chronological unfolding of the seven years in the form of the three series of judgments. In true Semitic style, history is moved forward a bit, then explanatory sections that flash both backwards and forwards in time are added. Then history is moved forward again, etc.

A WORD FROM THE OTHER VIEW

What are the evidences to support a concurrent view of the three series of judgments?

The Semitic Style Argument

Gundry says, "The universally acknowledged Semitic style of Revelation favors the second view, according to which the seals, trumpets, and bowls will find somewhat concurrent fulfillment."[5]

As we have seen, the Semitic style is evident in the historic-prophetic cameos. But it doesn't require a concurrent arrangement of judgments. This has to be established on other grounds, because it assumes the conclusion.

The Final Catastrophe Argument

Gundry again says, "Several specific considerations positively require us to believe that the seventh seal and the seventh trumpet bring us to the end of the Tribulation and that the seven bowls are clustered at the end. The sixth seal leads us to the final catastrophe of judgment when Christ returns, for the wrath of the Lamb is just about to strike the wicked, who are calling upon the rocks and mountains to hide them (6:12-17)."[6]

A careful comparison of the events of the seventh seal, seventh trumpet and seventh bowl reveals that nei-

[5]Gundry, op. cit. p. 75.

[6]Gundry, ibid. p. 76.

ther the last seal nor the last trumpet is at the end of the Tribulation.

To be sure, there are some terrible things that happen in the judgment of the sixth seal. The kings, the great men, the military commanders, the rich, the strong, the slave, and the free man do hide in the caves and mountains from God who sits on the throne, and from the wrath of the Lamb (Revelation 6:15–16).

But this very description proves that it cannot be the end of the Tribulation. Because at the end, men's hearts will be so hardened, and they will be so blinded by demonic influences (see 16:13–14) that they no longer hide in fear. As incredible as it is, the Scripture says that they will not hide, but they will unite their armies and *attack* the Lord Jesus Himself as He returns (19:17–19).

The scenes of Revelation 6:15–17 and 19:17–19 cannot happen anywhere near each other, because it will take considerable time for men's hearts to become so hard that they no longer fear God, but actually attack Him.

The seventh trumpet also does not take us to the absolute end of the Tribulation. Remember, the seventh trumpet introduces the seven bowl judgments. The previous six trumpet judgments before are still restrained to some degree.

The bowl judgments which God expressly says "finish" His wrath, and are the "last" of the judgments, are totally unrestrained and bring back the Lord Jesus.

Even if Gundry could prove the concurrent view of Revelation's judgments, he still faces a problem with Chapter 6, Verse 17, which says, " . . . for the great day of their wrath *has come*; and who is able to stand?"

This verse places God's wrath before the post-Tribulational Rapture, which fouls up Gundry's whole post-Tribulational scheme.

In order to overcome this embarrassing verb tense (the "has come" of Revelation 6:17), Gundry comes up with a very novel interpretation, "At first glance we might think that the divine wrath is placed in the past by a historical aorist. But if the wrath has already fallen, how could the wicked be yet fleeing for refuge? (The answer is because they know that there is more wrath to come. H.L.) Rather, the wrath is at the inception of its breaking forth (ingressive aorist) or on the verge of doing so (dramatic aorist)—'has just arrived' or 'is here'."[7]

It is true that an aorist tense verb in the Greek language, which pictures an action as happening at a point of time, can be viewed from three perspectives (past, near past, or occurring). However, to give an aorist a meaning other than past action is highly subjective on the interpreter's part and cannot be used as proof for a major argument. At best, it would be a supporting point.

I majored in New Testament Greek, had five academic years of study in it, and have studied it on my own for the past twenty-three years. So I know that Gundry's interpretation of this verb is not only highly subjective, but also not in accord with the mainstream of translators and commentators on this verse who had no axe to grind.

Ryrie comments on Gundry's interpretation of Revelation 6:17,

"To counter the force of this statement, posttribulationists have to understand the aorist as meaning that the wrath is on the verge of breaking forth, that is, it will not have started before the end. Now this is a possible use of the aorist, but highly unlikely in this verse. As Alford indicates, 'the virtually perfect sense of the aorist *elthen* here can hardly be questioned.' (Henry Alford, *The Greek New Testament*, 4 vols. (London: Rivington, 1875, 4:622)). He explains this sense of the aorist as 'alluding to the result of the whole series of events past, and not to be expressed in English except by a perfect' (4:665). Thus supported by reputable scholarship, the meaning of this verse is *not* that the wrath of God is on the verge of being poured out (as posttribulationists *must* understand it or spoil the system), but that the wrath has already been poured out with continuing results."[8]

SUMMARY

So we find that both the overall chronology of prophecy concerning the Tribulation, as well as the chronology of the book of Revelation, does not fit the post-Tribulational Rapture view. There is no way to cram all of the Divine wrath into the last moments of the Tribulation.

I believe, therefore, that we can trust God's promise in these days of ever-increasing turmoil, "For God has not destined us for *wrath*, but for obtaining salvation [deliverance] through our Lord Jesus Christ." (1 Thessalonians 5:9)

So we are to keep on believing God's promises, "and to wait for His Son from heaven, whom He raised from the dead, that is Jesus, who delivers us from the *wrath* to come." (1 Thessalonians 1:10)

[8]Charles C. Ryrie, *What You Should Know About The Rapture* (Chicago: Moody Press, 1981), p. 97.

SEVEN

OTHER RELEVANT
REVELATION PASSAGES

I discussed in the last chapter the many complex issues that are related to establishing the chronology of the book of Revelation. In this chapter, several other specific passages in the book which contribute to answering the Rapture question will be analyzed.

The Promise to the True Church

In Revelation 3:10 there is an extraordinary promise given to the church of Philadelphia. As is the case with all seven of the letters to the churches in Revelation Chapters 2 and 3, this letter obviously has an application which goes far beyond the time of the original addressees.

The *context* indicates that the promise applies to the end times of the Church. This is true first because the next verse says, "I am coming quickly; hold fast what you have, in order that no one take your crown." (Revelation 3:11) This verse has to refer to the coming of Christ for the Church because it uses a warning that is consistently associated with it in this book (see 22:7, 12, 20).

Second, Verse 11 also mentions rewards and the receiving of a crown. This is definitely to be given at the "Bema" or judgment seat of Christ. Paul speaks of receiving a crown on "that day" (2 Timothy 4:8). Peter speaks of the "unfading crown of glory" that will be given to faithful elders "when the Lord comes" (1 Peter 5:4). This definitely ties the context to the time of Christ's coming for the Church.

The third reason why this promise must apply to the end times of the Church is given in Verse 10 itself. The promise is said to apply to "that hour which is about to come upon the whole world, to test those who dwell upon the earth." So the time period concerns a test which God will send upon the whole world. It is obvious that such a global "test" has not yet occurred.

The What, Who, and Why of the Test

It is important to understand just *what* the original Greek word translated "test" means. The original word is *periazo*. Dr. Gingrich says that the word is used here in the sense of "to try, to make trial of, to put to the test, in order to discover or reveal what kind of a person someone is."[1] Often the purpose of the trial is to bring out the evil that is in someone. For this reason it is sometimes translated "temptation."

In this context it is best understood as putting the world under severe trial to reveal its evil heart. The trials are launched against "the whole inhabited earth," which is further defined as "those who dwell upon the earth." The apostle John makes this a technical descriptive clause to mark out a certain class of people.

[1] F. Wilbur Gingrich and Frederick Danker from Walter Bauer's 5th Edition, *A Greek-English Lexicon of the New Testament and Other Early Christian Literature* (Chicago: Univ. of Chicago Press, 1979), p. 640.

Listen to what John says about *those who dwell upon the earth*: (1) They are the ones who murder the Tribulation believers (6:10). (2) The wrath of God contained in the judgments called the "three woes" will specifically fall upon them (8:13). (3) They will murder the two special prophets of God (whom I believe will be Moses and Elijah) and rejoice over their deaths (11:10). (4) The message given by these two prophets will torment them (11:10). (5) They will worship the Roman Antichrist, and their names are not in the Lamb's book of life (13:8, 12). (6) They will be deceived by the miracles of the False Prophet from Israel (13:14). (7) They will be intoxicated and blinded by the false one-world religious system (17:2).

From this survey we can easily see *why* God is going to have *an hour* of testing for this group. It is to so demonstrate the hard, evil hearts of "those who dwell upon the earth" that God's judgment of them will be shown as totally just.

There is also a very important contrast in Revelation between "those who dwell upon the earth" and another special group called *"those who dwell in heaven."*

Let us first consider who "those who dwell in heaven" are. First, they cannot be angels because of a statement made in Revelation 12:12 about this same group of "heaven dwellers." It says, "For this reason, rejoice, O heavens and *you who dwell in them*, woe to the earth and the sea, because the devil has come down to you, having great wrath, knowing that his time is short." God's angels would not be exhorted to rejoice because they are not dwelling on earth during the devil's unrestrained wrath. Satan couldn't hurt them.

Second, this is not a reference to the departed souls of those massacred during the Tribulation. Though a nonresurrected believer's soul does go to be consciously with the Lord after he dies, he is never said "to dwell in heaven" until after he receives a resurrection body. Furthermore, it would make no sense for the devil to blaspheme the souls of those whose bodies he has just murdered.

Third, there is a direct contrast made between "those who dwell on earth," who are unbelievers, and "those who dwell in heaven." The implication is that the "heaven dwellers" are believers.

So the question is: If they are not believers, who are they? not angels, and they are

I believe the answer is that they are the translated (Raptured) saints of the Church who are now dwelling in heaven in glorified bodies. This explanation gives an intelligent reason for why the devil would take the time to blaspheme them. After all, he couldn't very well hide or sweep into a corner the news of millions of "Jesus freaks" disappearing. So Satan must give an explanation to his followers lest they slip into the other camp.

I believe the Holy Spirit has given us here a clear clue as to the whereabouts of the missing Church.

The Church of Philadelphia

The prophetic application of the letter to the Church in Philadelphia is to the *true Church* in the last stage of church history. It is to the *true Church* in the last stage of church which depicts the predominant *apostate church* of the last stage of church history.

It is to the true Church that God says, "Because you have kept the work of My perseverance, I also will keep you from the *hour* of testing, that *hour* which is about to come upon the whole inhabited earth [literal], to test those who dwell upon the earth." (Revelation 3:10)

Gingrich, quoting the great Greek scholar Walter Bauer, brings much light to the meaning of "the word of My perseverance." He says that it literally means "because you have kept the word concerning patient expectation of Me."[2] This would mean that the promise is to those who patiently expect the Lord's coming. If that is correct, it certainly would fit the context.

However, I believe that it also means that they have persevered in clinging to the truth of God's word under much opposition.

Now because of this perseverance, God promises, "I will keep you from the hour of testing that is coming upon the whole inhabited earth." The post-Tribulationist vigorously disputes the meaning of this promise. Some even try to make it have no clear meaning at all.

There are three important aspects to analyze in this promise. First, what does the word *keep* mean? Second, what does it mean to be kept *from the hour* of testing? Third, what length of time is meant by the term *"hour"*?

The verb "to keep" (*tereo* in Greek) means "to protect," in this instance according to Bauer.[3] God makes a solemn promise to those who are faithful to His Word. He says, "I will protect you . . ."

This protection is not just from the testing, but from the *time* of the testing. This is often overlooked by those who dispute the application of this verse. The major area of dispute is over the exact meaning of the preposition translated "from" which is the word *ek* in the original.

The Greek preposition *ek* in most circumstances means a separation from within something. There are only two instances in the New Testament where *ek* is used with the verb *tereo*. Both of them are in the writings of the apostle John.

The first instance is in John 17:15 where Jesus prayed for His disciples, "I do not ask Thee to take them out of

[2]Ibid. p. 846 (2).
[3]Ibid. p. 815.

the world, but to keep (*tereo*) them from (*ek*) the evil one." The idea is that Jesus wants the believer to be protected from falling under the authority of the evil one (Satan). It is clear that the disciples were not in Satan's clutches at the time Jesus prayed the prayer. So in this case *ek* used with *tereo* means to be protected from coming under Satan's power.

The only other instance these words are used together is here in Revelation 3:10. The same author, John, is expressing the same idea. He is saying that God will protect the believer **from the time** of the testing, not just from the testing.

The meaning of "the hour of worldwide testing" must be understood in the light of the main focus of the book of Revelation. Revelation specifically details the judgments, events and personalities of the seven years of Daniel's Seventieth Week. It begins with the worldwide deception and takeover by the Antichrist of Rome. It ends with the worst holocaust of all time. Its purpose is to bring the sons of Abraham, Isaac and Jacob to faith in the true Messiah and to judge the unbelievers from all nations called "those who dwell upon the earth." So "the hour" must apply to the whole seven-year Tribulation where all these things fall upon the world.

Search for the Missing Church

I mentioned briefly in the last chapter a very important piece of evidence in Revelation which supports that the Church is translated before the beginning of the Tribulation period.

The book of Revelation, which, as I've said, is the only book in the Bible specifically written to detail the events and phenomena of the Tribulation, nowhere mentions the Church as present on earth during the Tribulation. This point gains even more significance in the light of the fact that the Church is mentioned nineteen times in Chapters 1 through 3.

After the voice from heaven says to the apostle John, "come up here, and I will show you what must take place after these things" (Revelation 4:1), the Church vanishes from these earthly scenes.

Revelation makes continual reference to the believers who are on earth during this time, so there is every reason to expect that the term Church would be mentioned if these believers were the Church. There is one striking case where the Church certainly should have been mentioned if it were on earth.

There is a formula that is addressed to the Church seven times in Chapters 2 and 3. It says, "He who has an ear, let him hear what the Spirit says to the *Churches.*" (Revelation 2:7, 11, 17, 29; 3:6, 13, 22) This exact formula is repeated again during the Tribulation in Revelation 13:9 and 10, "If anyone has an ear, let him hear. If anyone *is destined* for captivity, to captivity he goes; if anyone kills with the sword, with the sword he must be killed. Here is the perseverance and the faith of the saints."

This is an extremely strong evidence for the Church's absence. In Chapter 13:9 the formula is given to alert Tribulational believers to hear and take heed to the life and death instructions to them of 13:10. In Verse 10, believers of that period are instructed not to resist being taken captive for their faith by the Antichrist, nor are they to resist with weapons. If they use weapons, God says that they will be killed by them.

Instead the believers are instructed to persevere in their faith in Jesus Christ and leave whether they die as martyrs or survive until the second advent up to the Lord.

Now this is a very clear situation where the term "church" should have been used because it is speaking to all the believers of that time about vital survival instructions. But even though the formula is exactly the same as the one given in Chapters 2 and 3, the word "church" is left out of Verse nine.

Church Appearances in Heaven

When the apostle John is caught up to heaven in Revelation Chapter 4, he sees *seven lamps of fire burning before the throne of God* (Verse 5). Those seven lamps first appeared on earth in Chapter 1, Verses 12 through 20. In Verse 20 they are identified as the seven symbolic churches. I believe that these seven lamps are the Church which has just been raptured into heaven. Here they are called the seven spirits of God because John is emphasizing that the Spirit indwells the churches.

The Bride in Heaven

The Church doesn't specifically reappear until just before the second coming of Christ to the earth in Revelation 19:7–16. As previously mentioned, the bride is in heaven already rewarded and prepared for the great wedding feast. The Lord Jesus Christ begins His second coming to earth.

The bride of Christ then accompanies Him to the earth on white horses wearing the white robes of her righteous deeds.

The post-Tribulationists have to go all out to try and explain away the sequence of events in this passage. Concerning this passage Ladd says, "So the vision of the bride prepared for the wedding feast is prophetic. *In vision,* John sees the bride ready for the marriage; but this is not a vision depicting either the saints in the intermediate state or the Church in heaven prior to the return of Christ. It is a vision of what shall be after Christ returns. Then will occur the resurrection of the dead in

Christ, both saints and martyrs (20:4). The final proof that this is a prophetic vision is the fact that the dead in Christ are not yet raised; their resurrection occurs after the return of Christ (20:4)."[4]

Ladd has not only to do violence to the immediate context of Revelation 19:7-16 to come up with such a farfetched interpretation, but he also has to do damage to the whole structure of the book of Revelation.

First of all, there is a chronological sequence of events in Revelation Chapter 19. The bride of Christ not only is seen in heaven already prepared for her wedding feast, but afterward the same bride returns with Christ in His second advent to earth (19:4).

Second, the book of Revelation moves through the Tribulation in a definite chronological order except for the interludes where the cameo sections explain the history and future of the personalities, organizations and events that culminate in the book. When Ladd says that John sees "the bride of Christ [the Church] *in vision*," he seems to think that this eliminates any necessity for following the normal, logical, chronological and temporal sequences that are established throughout the book. What Ladd doesn't recognize here is that the whole book of Revelation is a vision. But that doesn't remove the fact that the visions have a definite chronological sequence. If this logic were followed throughout the book, it would reduce it to an illogical, incoherent collection of visions that cannot possibly be understood.

Third, Ladd's own quote brings out the error of his interpretation. In fact, it is an extremely strong evidence for the Church's Rapture long before the second advent of Christ.

[4]George E. Ladd, *The Blessed Hope* (Grand Rapids: Wm. B. Eerdmans Pub. Co., 1956), p. 102.

An Embarrassing Resurrection

As previously quoted, Ladd says, "The final proof that this is a prophetic vision is the fact that the dead in Christ are not yet raised; their resurrection occurs after the return of Christ (20:4)."

Ladd seems to be so determined to prove his view that he must not have carefully evaluated the implications of the above statement.

First, if God intended for this book to be intelligible at all, Chapters 19 and 20 have a very definite chronological sequence: (1) Christ returns with His bride, the Church (19:7-16). (2) The armies of the Antichrist, the False Prophet and all the kings of the earth unite to fight Christ's return (19:19). (3) The Antichrist and the False Prophet are both taken and cast alive into the lake of fire (19:20). (4) All the rest of the armies with their kings are slain by Christ and given to the scavenger birds (19:21). (5) Satan is bound for a thousand years (20:1-3). (6) The martyred **Tribulation believers** are resurrected.

There is absolutely nothing in this context to indicate to an unbiased reader that this passage is anything other than a consecutive narrative of future history.

Now here is the point. Ladd agrees that this resurrection of **Tribulation saints** takes place **after** the return of Christ. If the Church is on earth during the Tribulation, and if the Church is raptured immediately *before* the second coming of Christ, then how is it that these Tribulation believers (who are the Church according to his view) are resurrected after the second coming? The Scripture says that "the dead in Christ shall rise first, then we who are alive and remain until the coming of the Lord shall be caught up together with them in the clouds to meet the Lord in the air." (1 Thessalonians 4:16-17)

If the Church were on earth and raptured just before the second coming (as post-Tribulationists must say), then all martyred Tribulation saints would be part of the Church and, therefore, have to be raised **before** the living believers could be translated into immortality. And all of this, according to post-Tribulationists, occurs just *before* the second advent.

This is a major evidence that the Church must be snatched up to meet the Lord long before the end of the Tribulation and the second advent.

Is God a Bigamist?

Gundry argues, "Israel is sometimes likened to a bride (Isaiah 49:18; 16:10; 62:5; Jeremiah 2:32; Hosea 2:19, 20) and the Church is likened to a wife (Ephesians 5:22–23). We should not expect to find rigid consistency in the Biblical use of metaphors. To press woodenly the marital relationship of both Israel and the Church to the Lord would be to say that God is a bigamist."[5]

Gundry's whole argument is misleading because Israel is never once said *to be* the bride of the Lord Jesus Messiah. God's attitude toward Israel is illustrated by various aspects of a bride's jewelry, by a bridegroom's excitement over his bride, and so forth.

But the Church is actually said to be the bride of Jesus Christ. In Ephesians 5:22–32, God says that though it is a great mystery, marriage is intended to be an earthly illustration of the believer's heavenly union with Christ. God says, ". . . because we are members of His body, of His flesh and of His bone. For this cause a man shall leave his father and his mother, and shall cleave to his wife; and the two shall become one flesh. This mystery

[5]Robert H. Gundry, *The Church and the Tribulation* (Grand Rapids: Zondervan Pub. House, 1973) p. 85.

is great; but I am speaking with reference to *Christ and the Church."* (Ephesians 5:30-32, NKJV)

The Hebrew marriage custom underlies the New Testament declaration of the Church as the bride of Christ. Ryrie traces the steps of the Hebrew marriage custom of that era,

"First, betrothal (which involved the prospective groom's traveling from his father's house to the home of the prospective bride, paying the purchase price, and thus establishing the marriage covenant); *second,* the groom's returning to his father's house and remaining separate from his father's house for twelve months during which time he prepared the living accommodations for his wife in his father's house; *third,* the groom's coming for his bride at a time not known exactly to her; *fourth,* his return with her to the groom's father's house to consummate the marriage and to celebrate the wedding feast for the next seven days (during which the bride remained closeted in her bridal chamber).

"In Revelation 19:7-9 the wedding feast is announced, which, if the analogy of the Hebrew marriage means anything, assumes that the wedding has previously taken place in the father's house. Today, the church is described as a virgin waiting for her bridegroom's coming (2 Corinthians 11:2); in Revelation 21 she is designated as the wife of the Lamb, indicating that previously she has been taken to the groom's father's house. Pre-Tributationists say that this requires an interval of time between the Rapture and the second coming."[6]

6Charles C. Ryrie, *What You Should Know About The Rapture* (Chicago: Moody Press, 1981), pp. 60-61.

All of the symbols and imagery used in the New Testament were based upon the common Hebrew culture of the day. Otherwise there would be no hope of understanding the rich use of parable, allegory and illustrations. Therefore, the standard Hebrew marriage tradition of that time gives insight into the Church as the bride of Christ, particularly in Revelation Chapters 19 and 21.

SUMMARY

I believe that these passages we have examined contribute significantly toward the case for a pre-Tribulation Rapture. The promise of being kept from the hour; the identity of those who dwell in heaven; the Church's absence from earth in Chapters 4 through 19; the bride's presence in heaven before the second coming, all fit into the pattern of a pre-Tribulation Rapture scenario.

Now let us look at the evidence in First and Second Thessalonians.

EIGHT

FIRST THESSALONIANS AND THE RAPTURE

The two New Testament letters that mention the Rapture were both written to the same people. These letters are First and Second Thessalonians.

These were the apostle Paul's earliest epistles. Both letters were written from Corinth in about the year A.D. 50, shortly after Paul's departure from Thessalonica (Acts 17:1–15 and 18:1–11).

Many important insights come from these early letters. *First*, it is nothing short of amazing how many Christian doctrines Paul taught these people who formed the church located in Thessalonica. He brought them from being idol-worshipping pagans to understanding the following major theological subjects in about four weeks: *election* (1 Thessalonians 1:4); *Holy Spirit* (1:5, 6; 4:8; 5:19); *assurance of salvation* (1:5); the *Trinity* (1:5, 6); *conversion* (1:9); the *Christian walk* (2:12; 4:1); *sanctification* (4:3; 5:23); *the day of the Lord* (5:1–3); the *three dimensions of man's nature* (5:23); *resurrection* (4:14–18); *Rapture of the Church* (1:10; 2:19; 3:13; 4:14–17;

5:9, 23); the *coming apostasy* (2 Thessalonians 2:3), the *advent of the Antichrist* (2 Thessalonians 2:3–12); the *second advent of Christ and world judgment* (2 Thessalonians 1:7–10).

These are only part of what Paul must have taught to them. Can you imagine today someone going to a city dominated by false religion, winning many to faith in Christ, founding a church, and then communicating all the above truths in four weeks? No wonder Paul said concerning his ministry there, "For our Gospel did not come to you in word only, but also in power and in the Holy Spirit and with full conviction . . ." (1 Thessalonians 1:5).

A *second* insight is that even though Paul had such a short time with them, he fully taught the whole scope of prophecy as it relates to the Rapture, the second coming of Christ and the world events that precede and follow. This fact alone should silence the many critical theologians and ministers who say that this subject is irrelevant to Christian living and shouldn't be taught. Paul had so thoroughly taught eschatology (prophecy) that he could refer to some advanced concepts and say, "Do you not remember that while I was still with you, I was telling you these things?" (2 Thessalonians 2:5).

The whole underlying occasion for writing these two letters sprang from the area of prophetic subjects. In First Thessalonians, Paul primarily answers the questions of whether believers who have died will be reunited with those who are still living at the time of the Rapture and are translated (1 Thessalonians 4:13–18).

In Second Thessalonians, Paul primarily writes to reassure the Thessalonian believers that they are not already in "the day of the Lord" and/or the Tribulation or the Seventieth Week of Daniel. (The first seven years of "the day of the Lord" coincides with the Tribulation period.)

Successful Living®

Book Mark

Thank you for buying this book! Please help us serve you better by completing and mailing this card!

___ I buy Successful Living books at ___

___ I've complimented the store manager for carrying these inspirational, family-type books!

___ Please send me your catalog.

___ I would appreciate spiritual counseling toward a more real and personal relationship with God.

___ I will support your ministry with prayer.

___ My church would like to have a rack.

___ Send details on how to be a Distributor.

___ Please send details on your Successful Living home party plan.

NAME _____

ADDRESS _____

_____ ZIP _____

PHONE (___) _____

". . . If you confess with your mouth, "JESUS IS LORD,' and believe in your heart that God raised HIM from the dead, you will be saved. For it is with your heart that you believe and are justified, and it is with your mouth that you confess and are saved." Romans 10:9,10 [New International Version]

WHAT IS SUCCESSFUL LIVING?

We're an organization which takes a **positive** action distributing inspirational books through dedicated independent Distributors. Want to participate? Mail this card today!

WHY THIS EMPHASIS?

"If religious books are not widely circulated among the masses in this country, I do not know what is going to become of us as a nation. If truth be not diffused, error will be; if God and His Word are not known and received, the devil and his works will gain the ascendancy; if the evangelical volume does not reach every hamlet, the pages of a corrupt and licentious literature will; if the power of the Gospel is not felt throughout the length and breadth of the land, anarchy and misrule, degradation and misery, corruption and darkness, will reign without mitigation or end."

—Daniel Webster, 1823

CALL OR WRITE TODAY!
Your Successful Living Distributor

GEORGE S. HIXSON, Distributor

(Successful Living Paperback Books)

1017 N. 25th St., K. C., Kansas 66102

Phone (913) 342-0847

The Problem of Lazy Brethren

A second occasion for writing both letters was the problem of those who misapplied the practical meaning of Paul's teaching concerning the "any moment" possibility of Christ's return which is commonly called the doctrine of imminence.

Two things should be observed about the way Paul dealt with this error. First, Paul doesn't deny or tone down his teaching that Christ's coming for the Church could be near. Some people think that no one should teach that Christ's coming could be very near because it could cause some to drop out of jobs, school, get married prematurely, and so forth, becoming generally irresponsible. However, the possible misapplication of a truth is never a justification for not teaching it. Some people misapply the truths of salvation, but we should continue to teach them.

Second, Paul shows that even if Christ were to come today, we should live responsibly and maintain a good testimony to the end. It has been my experience that most believers are motivated to greater dedication, faith, and spiritual production by the hope that the coming of the Lord Jesus approaches in their lifetime.

In 1 Thessalonians Paul reminds these idle believers of his example before them (2:9-10). He exhorts them to work, supply their own needs and maintain a testimony to the nonbelievers (4:11-12). Paul's first priority was to win people to Christ and to build them up in the faith. This, he tells us, is the proper response to the expectation of the Lord's imminent return.

The Rapture is mentioned in every chapter of 1 Thessalonians. The amazing emphasis of this doctrine in the earliest epistles underscores its importance.

The Rapture Delivers from Wrath
(1 Thessalonians 1:10)

Paul says in Chapter 1, "And to wait for His Son from heaven, whom He raised from the dead, that is Jesus, who delivers from the wrath to come." (1:10)

Dr. Morris comments on the term, *wait*, "The word for 'to wait' is found only here in the New Testament. And Grimm-Thayer (Greek dictionary) suggests that in addition to the thought of waiting for someone expected, it includes 'the added notion of patience and trust.' Finding it implies 'sustained expectation.'"[1]

This emphasizes that the believer is to constantly expect and await Christ's return. It is to be a primary motivating hope that inspires us to live for God and sustains us in adversity. The Thessalonians were undergoing extreme persecution. Paul reminds them that even though the present conditions are severe, the Lord will deliver us from the coming wrath of God upon the unbelieving world, which will be much more severe.

The purpose of this coming of "the Lord from heaven" is *to deliver* the true Church, composed of all believers, from this prophetic wrath to come. The verb "to deliver" is *ruomai* in the Greek. It means to deliver, rescue or save someone from a terrible situation in which he is helpless. This same term is used, for example, in Matthew 6:13 ("*deliver* us from evil") and in Colossians 1:13 ("He [Christ] *delivered* us from the domain of darkness"). This is a perfect term to describe the Rapture because it truly is a deliverance from human history's worst period of suffering.

[1]Leon Morris, *The First and Second Epistles to Thessalonians* (Grand Rapids: Eerdmans Pub. Co., 1959).

Rapture, Reunion, and Crown (2:19–20)

In Chapter 2, Paul says concerning the Rapture, "For who is our hope or joy or crown of exultation? Is it not even you, in the presence of our Lord Jesus at His coming? For you are glory and joy." (2:19, 20)

The apostle speaks of those whom he has introduced to Christ as his crown of exultation when the Lord Jesus comes in the Rapture. I believe that when the Rapture occurs we will be reunited with all those we helped come to faith in Christ. They will be part of our reward and crown at the Rapture. What a joyous thing to contemplate!

Rapture and an Unblamable Heart (3:12–13)

Paul says of the Rapture at the end of Chapter 3, " . . . May the Lord cause you to increase and abound in love for one another, and for all men, just as we also do for you; so that He may establish your hearts unblamable in holiness before our God and Father at the coming of our Lord Jesus with all His saints." (3:12–13)

If we allow the Holy Spirit to produce God's kind of love in us now, then we will have an unblamable heart of holiness when the Lord Jesus comes for the Church.

Paul also adds that all of the believers of the Church who have died will be with the Lord when He returns. This is explained in more detail in Chapter 4.

The Great Body Snatch (4:13–18)

Paul gives the basic reason for writing 1 Thessalonians at the end of Chapter 4. Since these verses have been commented on previously, it is sufficient to simply list the main points here.

First, believing loved ones who have died will not only join us in the Rapture, but will receive their resurrection bodies a split second before our translation. The Thessalonians were confused about whether they would see their loved ones again (4:13-15).

Second, the living believers will be snatched up bodily to meet the Lord and the departed saints in the air (4:16-17).

The Day of the Lord (5:1-11)

Paul answers another prophetic question that bothered the Thessalonians. He introduces this important section with the Greek phrase *peri de* ("Now as to" in NASB) which literally means "but concerning" or "now concerning." This was Paul's standard form for answering the questions of the ones to whom he was writing (see 1 Corinthians 1:11; 7:1; 7:25; 8:1; 12:1; 16:1). It always introduced a new subject and a new answer.

Let us read carefully the entire passage:

"Now as to the times and the epochs, brethren, you have no need of anything to be written to you. For you yourselves know full well that the day of the Lord will come just like a thief in the night. While they are saying, 'Peace and safety!' then destruction will come upon them suddenly like birth pangs upon a woman with child; and they shall not escape. But you, brethren, are not in darkness, that the day should overtake you like a thief; for you are all sons of light and sons of day. We are not of night nor of darkness; so then let us not sleep as others do, but let us be alert and sober. For those who sleep do their sleeping at night, and those who get drunk get drunk at night. But since we are of the day, let us be sober, having put on the breastplate of faith and love, and as a helmet, the hope of salvation. For God has not destined us for wrath, but for obtaining salvation through our Lord Jesus Christ, who died for us, that whether we are

awake or asleep, we may live together with Him.
Therefore encourage one another, and build up one
another, just as you also are doing." (1 Thessalonians
5:1–11)

The question concerned the "times" (*chronoi*) and "seasons" (*kairoi*) of prophetic events that precede and lead up to the Second Coming of the Lord (5:1). *Chronoi* refers to the specific times of prophetic events in chronological order. *Kairoi*, on the other hand, views the characteristics of the events themselves.

Paul's Answer

First, Paul reminds them that they already "know perfectly" about this subject (5:2). This stands in contrast to their ignorance about the subjects of the previous section (4:13–18).

Second, Paul groups their entire question about specific prophetic events and their characteristics under one all-inclusive prophetic period—"the day of the Lord." He had obviously taught them that the day of the Lord included all of the specific events that count down to the Lord's return once it began. So Paul focuses his answer on *how* and *under what world conditions* "that day" will begin. The following is a brief survey of what the Bible teaches about the day of the Lord.

Day of the Lord in Old Testament

This phrase is used about twenty times in the Old Testament. The parallel terms, "the last days" and "in that day" occur fourteen times and more than one hundred times, respectively. Walvoord says, "A study of numerous Old Testament references to the Day of the Lord and 'the Day', as it is sometimes called, should make it clear to anyone who respects the details of prophecy that the designation denotes *an extensive time of divine judgment on the world* (emphasis mine). Among the texts are Isaiah 2:12–21; 13:9–16; 34:1–8; Joel 1:15–2:11; 28–32; 3:9–12; Amos 5:18–20; Obadiah 15–17; Zephaniah 1:7–18." After a thorough study, Walvoord concludes, "Based on the Old Testament revelation, the Day of the Lord is a time of judgment, culminating in the second coming of Christ, and followed by a time of special divine blessing to be fulfilled in the millennial kingdom."[2]

Day of the Lord in the New Testament

Almost all the teaching concerning the Day of the Lord in the New Testament is in this passage and in 2 Thessalonians 2:1–12. The following is a summary of what these two passages teach about "the Day of the Lord."

First, it will come "like a thief in the night" upon the unbelieving world. This metaphor means that it will come with *surprise* and *suddenness.*

Second, it will come when the world is saying "peace and safety." When the Antichrist is revealed by being miraculously raised from a mortal wound (Revelation 13:3), he will give superhuman answers to the world that will be in a state of chaos. They will almost instantly receive him as world leader and rest in his pseudo-peace and safety.

Third, sudden destruction is associated with it. The judgments of the Day of the Lord will be like birth pangs seizing a pregnant woman (5:3). Once they begin, there is no escape. But they increase in frequency and severity until the birth is over. So it will be with these judgments which are also set forth in the book of Revelation.

Fourth, it begins shortly after the Antichrist is revealed, which is immediately after the removal of the

[2]John F. Walvoord, *The Blessed Hope and the Tribulation,* pp. 111, 113.

Holy Spirit's restraining ministry (2 Thessalonians 2:1–12). This passage connects the beginning of the Day of the Lord closely to the Antichrist's revelation.

Fifth, the Day of the Lord *will not* take the believers by surprise for two reasons. The first reason is because the believer is a child of light and of the day. This means that he has the illumination of the Holy Spirit and the prophetic Scripture (Daniel 12:8–10). Peter spoke of this very illumination, "For we did not follow cleverly devised tales when we made known to you the power and the coming of our Lord Jesus Christ, but we were eye-witnesses of His majesty . . . and so we have the prophetic word *made* more sure, to which you do well to pay attention as to a *lamp shining* in a dark place, until the *Day* dawns and the morning star arises in your hearts." (2 Peter 1:16, 19) So the believer will not be taken by total surprise. As I have taught many times, the believer will not know the day or the hour, but in these last days it has been revealed that he will know the general time (Matthew 24:32–36). However, if the believer of this economy were left in the Day of the Lord with all of its specific signs, he could calculate the day of the Lord's return.

The second reason that the Day will not overtake the believer like a thief is because "he is not destined for wrath, but for the obtaining of salvation through our Lord Jesus Christ" (5:9). We will be delivered from the wrath that begins with the Day of the Lord by the Rapture.

The post-Tribulationists have more problems than a one-armed paperhanger trying to fit the beginning of the Day of the Lord in at the very end of the Tribulation.

First, they have the problem of holding off all the Divine judgments until after the Rapture (which they say is simultaneous with the Second Advent), and then having them all fall before the Second Coming. This means that at least most of the trumpet and seal judgments, plus all of the bowl judgments, would have to occur in less than five minutes. This view would also have to compress the invasion of the king of the North (Daniel 11:40–45; Ezekiel 38–39) and the kings of the East (Revelation 16:12) into that short period.

Second, they have to explain why the unbelievers of that time will proclaim "peace and safety" (5:3) in the midst of all the concentrated wrath from God. "Peace and safety" is contrasted with the sudden destruction that follows. So Gundry's interpretation that they are only wishing for peace and safety doesn't make sense.

Third, the fear and concern the Thessalonians have about being already in the Day of the Lord (2 Thessalonians 2:1–5) cannot be reconciled with the post-Tribulation view. Unless "the Day" started near the time of the Antichrist's unveiling, the passage wouldn't make sense. It would have been obvious to the Thessalonians that they could not be in the Day of the Lord if it were only at the very end.

All of us must admit that there are some things that are difficult to reconcile on this issue. But the pre-Tribulation view harmonizes all of the scriptural evidence best, and answers the most questions satisfactorily.

Sanctified and Complete at the Rapture (5:23–24)

Paul mentions the Rapture again in his closing prayer for the Thessalonians.

Paul prays, "May God Himself, the God of peace, sanctify you through and through. May your whole spirit, soul and body be kept blameless at the coming of our Lord Jesus the Messiah. The one who calls you is faithful and he will do it." (5:23, 24 NIV)

Paul reveals a beautiful truth in this prayer. It is God who sanctifies us. The verb "to sanctify" (*hagiazo* in the

Greek) has a common root with the term "holy." It literally means to set something apart as God's possession and for God's use. The word was used in ancient Greece even to describe inanimate objects that were offered to the ancient temple gods.

Paul's prayer is that God will progressively set apart our whole being to Himself. Paul then gives a promise of assurance that God will see that this is accomplished in our lives because *He* is faithful. The end result is that we will be blameless when we are caught up to stand before our Lord Messiah in the Rapture.

SUMMARY OF 1 THESSALONIANS

In conclusion, the following principles are taught in 1 Thessalonians concerning the Rapture:

(1) The doctrine of the Rapture was taught even to young believers.

(2) The Rapture will deliver believers in the Lord Jesus from the predicted time of wrath which is part of the beginning of the "Day of the Lord" (1:10; 5:9).

(3) All living believers will be suddenly caught up to meet the Lord in the air, and will be reunited with loved ones who have died.

(4) The believer will have an awareness of the general time of the Rapture's approach (5:4–5).

(5) The Day of the Lord will come with sudden destruction upon the unsuspecting, nonbelieving world while it is proclaiming peace and safety (5:2–3). The Rapture delivers believers from this period of destruction, as we noted in (2).

(6) The hope of the Rapture and its deliverance

from wrath is to be a source of comfort and encouragement to the believer (1:10; 4:18 and 5:11).

As the world spins virtually out of control from crisis to crisis, this hope burns ever brighter. May the impact of the incredible promises of deliverance from wrath we have just studied not be lost in the technical details.

NINE

LIGHT FROM A FORGED LETTER

Second Thessalonians contains a very important passage with regard to the chronology of events related to the Rapture. Whether you are a pre-, mid-, or post-Tribulationist, the interpretation of this letter is crucial.

The apostle Paul clearly states his main reason for writing the letter in Chapter 2, Verses 1 and 2:

"Now we request you, brethren, with regard to the coming of our Lord Jesus Christ, and our gathering together to Him, . . .

"That you may not be quickly shaken from your composure or be disturbed either by a spirit or a message or a letter as if from us, to the effect that the Day of the Lord has come." (2 Thessalonians 1–2)

The phrase "as if from us" brings out the real problem that this letter seeks to correct. Someone had brought a message to them, representing it as from Paul, which said that the Day of the Lord had already begun.

Paul begins to correct this grave error by appealing to "the coming of the Lord Jesus Christ." He specifies carefully which aspect of His coming by the qualifying clause "and our gathering together to Him . . . ." This could only refer to the Rapture when all Christians will be caught up to be with Christ.

Because Paul begins this important section of the letter by holding up the promise of the Rapture first, it is obvious that it has an important bearing on whether the Day of the Lord has indeed already come.

The fact that Paul holds up the Rapture as yet to occur seems to remind the Thessalonians of its chronological relationship to the Day of the Lord. Since the Rapture hasn't occurred, the Day of the Lord could not already be present.

The Terrifying Forgery

Two words describe the Thessalonians' reaction to the forged message. The first is the verb *saleuo*, which is translated "shaken." It means to shake or agitate something. It is a violent term that is used sometimes to describe an earthquake. We have a slang expression today that captures this idea. We say, "He's all shook up," meaning that someone is thoroughly shaken from his emotional moorings. The people had been shaken from what they had been taught and become thoroughly confused.

The second term describing the impact of the forgery is translated "disturbed." The original Greek word (*throeo*) means "to be frightened." It is in the present tense which means that they were in a *continuing state of fear.*

Gundry disagrees with this premise. He says that the Thessalonians were only a little agitated, not fearful. He also says that their agitation was due to some believers who had erroneously understood that the Lord's coming was near and had quit their jobs. This misses the point of the context altogether. The Thessalonians were in a state of fear, not just agitated. They were confused and fearful because they thought they were already in the Tribulation, not because a few quit their jobs.

A CRUCIAL QUESTION

The following question helps reveal what Paul must have taught them. If Paul had told them that the Rapture followed the Day of the Lord, these people would not have been troubled but rather rejoicing because the Lord's coming for them would have been very near. They would have faced the Tribulation with hope and steadfastness, knowing that the Rapture was less than three and one-half years away, if Paul had taught a mid-Tribulation Rapture, or less than seven years away if he had taught a post-Tribulation Rapture.

But, if Paul had instructed them that the Rapture preceded the Day of the Lord, and afterwards a forged message was received that said they were already in that Day, then their panic becomes completely understandable.

I believe this scenario best explains the conditions that underlie this epistle. This whole context reflects that Paul had taught them a pre-Tribulation scenario for the Rapture.

Paul sets up a threefold denial of any message from himself which said that the Day of the Lord had come. He lists the three different ways that a false message could have been communicated, and denies them all. He sent neither a spirit, nor a verbal message, nor a written letter with such a teaching. Paul's usual way of communication was a written letter. For this reason he urges them to check out any letter presented as being from him by verifying his handwritten greeting and signature (3:17-18). He also wanted them to know that this letter correcting the forgery was not itself a forgery.

Two Imperative Historical Signs

Paul reminds them of two world-shaking events of prophecy which must happen just before the Day of the Lord can begin. He obviously selects these two events because they are of such magnitude that they could not occur unnoticed. About this Paul says,

"Let no one in any way deceive you, for it [the Day of the Lord] will not come unless the apostasy comes first, and the man of lawlessness is revealed, the son of destruction, who opposes and exalts himself above every so-called god or object of worship, so that he takes his seat in the temple of God, displaying himself as being God.

"Do you not remember that while I was still with you, I was telling you these things?" (2 Thessalonians 2:3-5)

The Great Apostasy

The first event which precedes the Day of the Lord is "the apostasy." This word (*apostasia* in Greek) means to deliberately forsake and rebel against known truth from and about God.

The definite article before the term "apostasy" clearly indicates that it is a definite event, not just a progressive rebellion. The article also points out that this fact had been taught to them before.

There are many New Testament warnings about a progressive apostasy in the last days which would grow in intensity within professing Christendom. Apostasy was perceptible even in the early Church as shown in Verse 7 where it is called "the mystery of lawlessness." But "the apostasy" is a reference to a climactic event when the professing church will completely revolt against the Bible and all of its historical truths.

This ultimate act of apostasy on the part of professing Christendom sets the stage for the second great sign, which apparently happens almost simultaneously.

The Unveiling of the Antichrist

With all restraint of lawlessness removed (that is, the rejection of God and His Truth), the door is opened for Satan to reveal his masterpiece, the Antichrist. He is called here "the man of lawlessness" and "the son of destruction." The exact meaning of these titles is "the man who brings lawlessness" and "the son who brings destruction."

What accurate insight these two descriptive titles give us. The Antichrist, who will spring forth from the modern remains of the ancient Roman culture and people, will cause the worst period of lawlessness and destruction the world has ever seen.

Daniel's prophecies about this world dictator give more insight into this aspect of his awesome career,

"And he will speak out against the Most High and wear down the saints of the Highest One, and he will intend to make alterations in **times** *and in* **law;** *and they will be given into his hand for a time, [and two] times, and half a time [three and one-half years]."* (Daniel 7:25)

"And in the latter period of their rule [Gentile world power], when the transgressors have run their course, a **king** *will arise insolent and skilled in intrigue.*

"And **his** *power will be mighty, but not by his own power [he will have Satan's powers], and he will* **destroy** *to an extraordinary degree and prosper and perform his will; he will destroy mighty men and the holy people.*

"And through his shrewdness he will cause deceit to succeed by his influence; and he will magnify himself in his heart, and he will **destroy many by means of peace . . ."** *(Daniel 8:23-25a)*

These Scriptures teach us that the Antichrist will alter times and laws to his own purpose. He will also be a master of deceit, and will deceive the whole world into following him. While capitalizing on the world's desire for *peace and security* (1 Thessalonians 5:3), he will bring them under his control and to ultimate destruction.

Paul gives a threefold summary of this Messianic counterfeit.

First, he opposes and exalts himself above every so-called god or object of worship. The Antichrist will seek to destroy all truth about God and even the gods of other religions.

Second, he will take his throne into the holy of holies of the third Jewish temple which must be rebuilt upon its ancient site.[1] This act will fulfill Daniel's and Jesus' prophecy concerning the "abomination of desolation" which officially begins the last three and one-half years of the Tribulation period (Daniel 9:27 compared with Matthew 24:15).

Third, he will proclaim and display himself as being God. This is the ultimate blasphemy. He will take secular humanism into the religious sphere by deifying man.

[1] It has recently been discovered that the holy of holies lies approximately 100 meters north of the Dome of the Rock. This means that the third temple could now be built without disturbing the third holiest Muslim shrine.

He will not only deceive the world into accepting him as the supreme political dictator, but will also demand worship (Revelation 13:4 and 15).

A Necessary Prelude

Another line of prophetic chronology makes it absolutely necessary for these two events to precede the Day of the Lord. This was previously mentioned briefly, but bears repeating here.

The Roman Dictator must be unveiled a short while before the actual beginning of Daniel's Seventieth Week, which also begins the Day of the Lord. This is necessary because, as stated before, it begins with the signing of a guarantee of protection for Israel between the Roman Dictator of the revived Roman Empire, and the leader of Israel called the False Prophet. The Roman Antichrist must have time to be revealed, take over the ten-nation European confederacy and establish himself as a world leader before he can have a power base from which to make the convenant with the Israeli leader.

Such momentous events necessitate an interlude between the revelation of the Antichrist and the official beginning of the Day of the Lord.

The Restrainer

After reminding the Thessalonians of the two signs just mentioned, Paul takes up another prophetic personality of whom he assumes their previous knowledge.

The apostasy and the Antichrist refer to future events. The conditions described by "the Restrainer" relate to the present time and to what is holding back these two fateful events.

Paul admonishes them by saying,

"And you know **what restrains** *him [Antichrist] now, so that in his time he may be revealed.*

*"For the mystery of lawlessness [apostasy] is already at work; only **He who now restrains** will keep on doing so until **He is taken out of the way.***

"And then that lawless one will be revealed . . . "
(2 Thessalonians 2:6–8a)

The apostle had taught this subject so well that he could say "you know." Then he refers to the most critical subject of the whole context, "the Restrainer."

The term for "restrainer" (*katexo*) literally means to hold down or suppress something. It is translated in this sense in Romans 1:18 where it speaks of the unbeliever suppressing the truth.

In Verse 6, the Restrainer is called an influence by the use of the neuter gender in the participle form of the verb to restrain. But in Verse 7 a singular masculine gender is used to describe the Restrainer, thus showing that he is also a person.

The Duration of the Restrainer's Mission

The apostle Paul said that the Restrainer would keep on restraining both the mystery of lawlessness and the advent of the man of lawlessness continuously until **He** literally "takes Himself out of the midst." (This translation is demanded by the middle voice of the Greek verb.) Immediately after the Restrainer removes Himself from His mission, the Antichrist will be revealed.

Now let us list the characteristics of the Restrainer.

First, the Restrainer must be both a worldwide influence and a person. This suggests omnipresence.

Second, the Restrainer must be a supernatural person to be able to restrain from Paul's time to the present hour.

Third, the Restrainer must be a powerful person to

hold back two such mighty forces as worldwide apostasy and the Antichrist's advent.

Fourth, the Restrainer must have some logical reason for *terminating* the restraint of lawlessness and the Antichrist's advent, which agrees with the Biblical record.

Fifth, the Restrainer must have a logical reason to re-strain *lawlessness* and the man of lawlessness.

WHO IS THE RESTRAINER?

There have basically been three different major views as to who or what "the Restrainer" is.

Is the Restrainer Human Government?

Some have said that the Restrainer is *human government*. Those who held this view in past history were not generally noted for their adequate view of the prophetic Scripture.

Mary Stewart Relfe is one of the modern-day Bible teachers who holds this view. She says,

"The Church was already in severe persecution at the hands of Rome, so Paul chose not to invite more suffering by naming the Roman power. He had previously in person identified it. Rome was so powerful that Paul knew *another* Super World Dictator professing to be above all could not rise to power until Rome was removed. Likewise, we know this power which has prevented the reveal-ing of the Wicked One has been subsequent gov-ernment structures.

"When the government of the world becomes un-able to enforce law and order (or 'is taken out of the way'), this condition will give rise to the revela-tion of this Wicked One World Leader, who will himself bring about some semblance of law and order. He will be revealed to the Christians in 2 Thessalonians 2:3 at the outset of the last seven years, but his wickedness will not be revealed to the world until midweek."[2]

There are a number of problems with this view. In fact Relfe's statement quoted above has some inner contradictions. This view must be rejected for the following reasons:

(1) It doesn't adequately explain the use of the masculine gender for the Restrainer in Verse 7 (*o katechon* in Greek). If the Restrainer were an impersonal force, the neuter gender would have continued to be used as in Verse 6. The deliberate switch to the masculine singular in Verse 7 indicates that the Restrainer is definitely a person.

(2) Human government doesn't have enough power to restrain Satan, who is second in power and intelligence only to God. Nor does it have the power or a logical reason for restraining "the mystery of lawlessness" which we have previously seen is that progressive development of the rejection of God and His truth. To say that the wicked Roman Empire, or any other form of human government, has restrained Satan's relentless attack against God's truth borders on the preposterous.

Furthermore, the Scripture teaches that Satan and his demons rule over this present world system, and apart from God's gracious restraint, they manipulate and guide unbelieving government leaders (see Ephesians 2:1–3; cp. Daniel 10:12, 13).

The thing that truly baffles me is how Relfe can say, "Rome was so powerful that Paul knew *another* Super World Dictator professing to be above all *could not rise* to power until Rome was removed."[3] This doesn't make sense. First of all, Satan could have simply taken possession of the Caesar of that day and made him the Antichrist. How in the world could the Roman government, a human power, have prevented Satan, a superhuman person with awesome powers, from doing this? Second, the government that the coming Dictator will take over is a revived form of the old Roman Empire.

(3) This view doesn't explain adequately the reason for "the restrainer getting Himself out of the midst." Human government will reach its zenith under the Antichrist. Human government doesn't end until the second coming of Jesus the Messiah to set up God's kingdom on earth. And, human government can't get itself out of the way as the translation of the verb's middle voice requires.

This view just doesn't harmonize with the Bible as a whole, nor answer the demands of this context.

Is the Restrainer Satan?

Another view is that the Restrainer is Satan. This would fit the need of the Restrainer to be both an influence and a person. It could also explain the purpose clause of Verse 6 which says, "so that in his [the Antichrist's] time he may be revealed." The idea (in this

[3]Ibid.

view) is that Satan would restrain the Antichrist's revelation until the most opportune time in order to insure his successful reception.

Hogg and Vine, who hold this view, interpret Verse 7 as follows,

> *"Until he be taken;* as shown in the notes, there is nothing in the text to justify *taken. Ginomai* means to become, to come to be. Naturally then, the meaning of the phrase is to come into being, or to appear, rather than to be removed, or to disappear."[4]

Hogg and Vine go on to make the following amplified translation of Verses 7 and 8 to support their view,

> "For the secret of (the spirit of) lawlessness is already working; only (there is) the Controller at present (who will hold it in check) until he (the man of lawlessness) may become (successfully manifested) out of the very midst (of the situation that will develop, so not risking defeat by a premature attempt to capture the key position). And then (but not until then) the Lawless One shall be revealed whom the Lord Jesus shall slay, etc."[5]

There are serious flaws in this view. First, the normal meaning of the Greek term, *katecho,* is to restrain or suppress something that is in active opposition to the restraint.

Second, the clear meaning of Verse 7 is that the Restrainer is an obstacle to "the mystery of lawlessness," not an ally holding it in tactical check.

[4]C. F. Hogg and W. E. Vine, *The Epistles to the Thessalonians,* p. 242.
[5]Ibid.

Third, the antecedent of "*He* is taken out of the way" is clearly the Restrainer. To make the "he" refer to the Antichrist rather than the natural antecedent is grammatically extremely improbable.

This view doesn't agree with the simple meaning of the context. The most serious flaw of this view in the light of the context is that it makes Satan be in opposition to himself. About that situation Jesus said on another occasion, "Every kingdom divided against itself will be ruined, and every city or household divided against itself will not stand. If Satan drives out Satan, he is divided against himself. How then can his kingdom stand?" (Matthew 12:26–27, NIV)

Is the Restrainer the Holy Spirit?

The third major view is that the Restrainer is *the Holy Spirit*. Relfe takes strong exception to this, "The recent pre-trib doctrine teaches that this 'he' is the Holy Spirit. There are many blatant inconsistencies which render this untrue."[6]

With due respect, this is not a *recent* view. Some noted early Church leaders believed that the Holy Spirit is the Restrainer. Alford, in Volume III of his scholarly commentaries, mentions the following men on pages 57 and 58 (I am indebted to Gundry for this insight). The first was John of Constantinople who was also known as Chrysostom (A.D. 347–407). He was called Chrysostom (golden mouth) because of the eloquence of his preaching. He is known to history as the greatest Greek-speaking Christian preacher of all time.[7] A second early Church leader who believed this view was Theodore of

[6]Relfe, op. cit. p. 216.

[7]Earle E. Cairns, *Christianity Through the Centuries*, pp. 151–153.

Mopsuestia (A.D. 350–428).[8] And another was Theodoret, Bishop of Cyprus (A.D. 390–457).[9]

Gundry says in favor of the Spirit's restraining role, "Far from being novel, the view just might reflect apostolic teaching . . . the charge of novelty against this view, as we have seen, does not survive investigation. We may ask why Paul should not have openly mentioned the Holy Spirit. But what reason would have prompted him to do so? For they knew what he was writing about (Verses 5 and 6a). No other passage of Scripture teaches that the Spirit holds back the appearance of the Antichrist. But neither does any other Scripture teach that Satan, the Roman Empire, or human government holds back the Antichrist."[10]

Interpreting God the Holy Spirit as the Restrainer best answers the grammatical, contextual and theological questions involved in 2 Thessalonians for the following reasons:

(1) It best answers the usage of both the neuter and masculine singular gender to describe the Restrainer. The Spirit is a worldwide restraining power, which explains the use of the neuter gender. Furthermore, since the Greek word for spirit *(pneuma)* is neuter, the neuter pronoun is regularly used to refer to Him. However, the distinct personality of God the Spirit is also frequently emphasized in the same context with the neuter by referring to Him with the masculine singular gender (see John 15:26 and 16:13–14).

(2) The Holy Spirit is almost always referred to by

[8]Ibid. p. 153.

[9]Henry Bettenson, *The Early Christian Fathers.*

[10]Robert H. Gundry, *The Church in the Tribulation*, pp. 125–126.

a title that describes His particular function or ministry. For instance, He is called "the Spirit of Truth" (John 14:17); "the Helper" (John 16:17); "the Spirit of life in Christ Jesus" (Romans 8:2). These titles mean the Spirit who teaches truth, gives us help and empowers us with the life of Jesus. So it is very normal for Paul to simply refer to Him as the Restrainer to people that he had thoroughly taught on the matter.

(3) This view is also the most consistent with the Holy Spirit's historic role revealed in the Bible. Theologically, the third person of the Trinity, the Spirit of God, is the active agent in implementing the common plan of the Triune God. For instance, He is the active agent in God's program of creation and salvation.

(4) It takes a person of superior power to restrain a supernatural person and his superhuman program. Jesus called Satan "the *ruler* of this world [-system]" (John 14:30). And in another place it says that the unbeliever is under Satan's authority and control, "In which you formerly walked according to the spirit of this age, according to the *prince* of the power of the atmosphere [of thoughts and customs], of the *spirit* that is now energizing the sons of disobedience." (Ephesians 2:2, literally translated.)

Satan has a highly organized army of fallen angels that are called demons. It is through this means that he exercises worldwide power in programs such as "the mystery of lawlessness." God reveals about this world-governing system, "For our struggle is not against flesh and blood, but against the *rulers*, against the *powers*, against the *world forces* of [behind] this darkness, against the *spiritual forces* of wickedness in the heavenly places." (Ephesians 6:12)

Satan even has his own corps of dedicated ministers within the Church who are spreading the mystery of lawlessness, "For such men are false apostles, deceitful workers, disguising themselves as *apostles* of Christ. And no wonder, for even Satan disguises himself as an angel of light. Therefore it is not surprising if his *servants* also disguise themselves as *servants of righteousness* . . ." (2 Corinthians 11:13–15)

To say that human government could restrain these things is ludicrous. Satan has no logical reason to do so. The person of the Spirit of God is the only one with the motive and the power to confront such a person and his system.

(5) This view best explains the purpose clause, "so that in his time he [Antichrist] may be revealed" (Verse 6). The verb "to be revealed or unveiled" *(apokalupto)* is used three times in this context, each time in the passive voice. This indicates that the Antichrist is revealed by God's permission into his fateful historic role.

ANOTHER PROBLEM

Even though the Holy Spirit is definitely the Restrainer of 2 Thessalonians Chapter 2, there is another issue to settle.

There are two possible ways of viewing the Holy Spirit's ministry as Restrainer. One is that He restrains directly and personally apart from the Church. The other way is that He restrains through the agency of His present personal residence in the Church.

As might be expected, Gundry leads the few who hold to a personal and direct restraining role of the Spirit apart from the Church. (I think it is important to say to the reader at this point that though I have taken personal exception to Gundry throughout this book, it is done with a healthy respect for his evident spirituality and scholarship.)

Gundry observes, "We have no warrant to infer from the residence of the Holy Spirit in the Church that He cannot work independently from the Church or that He limits Himself to the Church as His sole sphere or medium of activity. Neither in the present passage nor in any other do we catch so much as a hint that restraint of the Antichrist and of the mystery of lawlessness forms one of the purposes for the Spirit's residence in the Church."[11]

Actually, I believe that Gundry misses part of the issue in his statement. I agree that the Holy Spirit, being an omnipresent and omnipotent person, cannot be limited to working *only* through the Church in which He personally dwells.

The Holy Spirit through the Church does exercise a restraint upon the world. We are both the *salt* that preserves and the *light* that illuminates the world.

But equally important is whether there are certain ministries the Holy Spirit performs in the world because the Church *is still in the world.* When Jesus first predicted the birth of the Church, He promised, ". . . upon this rock [that is, the profession of faith in Him as the son of God and Messiah] I will build My church; and the gates of Hell shall not overpower it. I will give you the keys of the kingdom of heaven; and whatever you shall bind on earth shall be bound in heaven, and whatever you shall

[11]Ibid. pp. 126–127.

loose on earth shall be loosed in heaven." (Matthew 16:18–19)

If the post-Tribulationists are correct, and the Church does go through the seven years of Tribulation, then this promise cannot be kept. First, the Holy Spirit stops restraining Satan and his activities. Second, the mystery of lawlessness is allowed to go rampant and the great apostasy takes place. Third, the Roman Antichrist is unveiled. Fourth, the Antichrist is given complete authority over believers: "And it was given to him [Antichrist] to make war with the saints and to *overcome* them: and authority over every tribe and people and tongue and nation was given to him." (Revelation 13:7)

There is no way to reconcile the above prophecy with the promise given to the Church, if these saints are from the Church. If the Church is on the earth during this period, Satan and his Antichrist will totally overpower it.

Furthermore, Jesus made another solemn promise to the Church that is even stronger, "All authority has been given to Me in heaven and on earth. Go therefore and make disciples of all the nations, baptizing them in the name of the Father and the Son and the Holy Spirit, teaching them to observe all that I commanded you; and *lo I am with You always, even to the end of the age.*" (Matthew 28:18–20)

In the light of this promise, it is a Divine necessity for the Holy Spirit to restrain apostasy and the Antichrist until the end of this Church age, which terminates with the evacuation of the Church. Otherwise, the Church would have been wiped out long ago.

All of the things which occur during the Tribulation are consistent with this view. The Tribulation becomes the hour of the power of darkness. The false apostles and ministers within the false church throw away all truth from God's Word and embrace the Antichrist as their leader. There is no more restraint. The world will be totally under Satan's authority.

The Holy Spirit will still work as He did in the Old Testament. He will not be gone from the world, but His unique ministries in, through and for the believer will be removed with the Church.

Relfe erects a straw man concerning this issue and then tears it down in her abrasive style, "If the church is to be raptured before the Tribulation, and 'he' the Holy Spirit is taken out at this time, as pre-trib espouses, how would those many Tribulation Saints with whom Antichrist makes war (Daniel 7:21; Revelation 13:7) get converted?"[12]

No informed exponent of pre-Tribulationism believes what she attributes to them. The Holy Spirit will endow the 144,000 chosen Israelites with the same kind of power He did the prophets in the Old Testament. In fact, two of the mightiest prophets from the economy of law will return to shake up the world. The Holy Spirit will convince men of their need of salvation, bring them to faith and regenerate them as He did from the beginning of man's sin.

But the unique Church economy ministries of indwelling, baptizing, sealing, gifting and filling of every believer will be removed with the Church. This is consistent with all that is revealed of the average Tribulational believer's level of spiritual insight, knowledge and maturity.

Gundry rejects this idea of a "reversal of Pentecost." He says that since all these ministries of the Spirit were given on the basis of the finished work of Christ, they cannot be removed.

But there is nothing in Scripture that says the conditions of one economy cannot be removed for a greater

<hr>

[12]Relfe, op. cit. pp. 216–217.

Divine purpose that has been predicted, and then returned at a later date.

This point is graphically illustrated by another similar Divine action. The whole system of animal sacrifice required by the Mosaic Law economy is set aside in this present economy. The writer of the epistle to the Hebrews shows point by point how this system was fulfilled in the one sacrifice of the Messiah Jesus. Yet we find in Ezekiel Chapter 40 that animal sacrifice will be reinstituted in a memorial sense during the one-thousand-year millennial kingdom.

Since the Tribulation is the final seven years of Daniel's prophecy of seventy weeks of years, and since the first sixty-nine weeks of years were under the conditions of the Mosaic Law economy, it stands to reason that the same conditions must return for the final week. Thus the present ministries of the Spirit must be removed.

The Purpose of the Day of the Lord (2:8–12)

The purpose of the Day of the Lord is the last part of Paul's argument that proves it has not yet come. Paul says, "And then [after the Restrainer and the Church are removed] the lawless one will be revealed, whom the Lord Jesus will overthrow with the breath of his mouth and destroy by the splendor of his coming. The coming of the lawless one will be in accordance with the work of Satan displayed in all kinds of counterfeit miracles, signs and wonders, and every sort of evil that deceives those who are perishing. They perish because they refused to love the truth [the Bible] and so be saved. For this reason *God sends them powerful delusions* so that they will believe *the lie* and so that all will be condemned who have not believed the truth but have delighted in wickedness." (2 Thessalonians 2:8–12, NIV)

After the Restrainer is taken out of the way, Satan will be allowed not only to bring in the Antichrist, but to counterfeit the miracles of Messiah Jesus through him. The same three words that are used to describe our Lord Jesus' miracles throughout the Gospels are used in Verse 9 to describe Satan's activity through the Antichrist.

The Beginning of God's Wrath

Both the mid-Tribulationists and the post-Tribulationists argue that God's wrath doesn't come upon the world until late in the Tribulation. As mentioned before, all three views agree that God promised the Church would not experience His wrath.

Because of this, the mid-Triber says that God's wrath doesn't begin until the last three and one-half years of the Tribulation. The post-Triber maintains that God's wrath doesn't fall until the very end of the Tribulation. Both of these positions are predicated on the assumption that God's wrath is only expressed *in a physical judgment.*

I believe that this passage predicts the wrath of God is poured out in *the spiritual realm* to a horrifying degree with the very outset of the Tribulation. (Physical wrath follows shortly after.)

Just look at the terrifying direct judgments of God noted in this passage:

(1) Satan is allowed by God to counterfeit the miracles of the Lord Jesus in order to deceive the world into following the Antichrist. (If this isn't an expression of Divine wrath, what is?)

(2) The unbelieving world will be opened to "every sort of evil that deceives those who are perishing" (Verse 10).

(3) ***God sends*** them a powerful delusion so that

they will believe *the lie*." (Verse 11) "The lie" probably refers to the Antichrist's claim to be God. This is a direct expression of wrath from God upon the whole world.

These expressions of God's wrath in the spiritual realm are much more terrifying to me than any of those predicted for the physical realm. Those who disagree need to hear the words of Jesus who said, "And do not fear those who kill the body, but are unable to kill the soul; but rather fear Him who is able to destroy both soul and body in hell." (Matthew 10:28)

PAUL'S FINAL PROOF

Paul assures the Thessalonians that they are not in the Day of the Lord because its purpose is to deceive and bring to destruction all those who rejected his truth and the Gospel. Since they have received and believed the truth, that Day is not for them. They will be removed with the Restrainer before the two events that set the stage for the Day of the Lord to begin.

Paul closes his argument with God's purpose for the believer, "But we should always give thanks to God for you, brethren beloved by the Lord, because God has chosen you from the beginning for salvation through sanctification by the Spirit and faith in the truth. And it was for this He called you through our gospel, that you may gain the glory of our Lord Jesus Christ." (2 Thessalonians 2:13–14) We should always be praising the Lord for His grace that has delivered us from the wrath that is soon to come.

In conclusion, the Thessalonian letters teach believers that God has not destined us for wrath, for Jesus is going to deliver us from the wrath to come (1 Thessalonians

5:9 and 1:10). But God has called us to gain the glory of our Lord Jesus Christ (2 Thessalonians 2:14).

In these days of growing darkness, what greater hope can we focus our hearts upon than these promises. The Rapture, thank God, is not a hope for the dead, but for the living.

INTERLUDE BETWEEN RAPTURE AND BEGINNING OF THE TRIBULATION

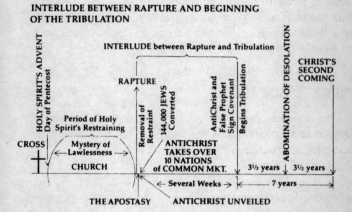

TEN

WHO WILL POPULATE
THE KINGDOM?

The most difficult question for post-Tribulationists to answer is: Who will populate the Millennial Kingdom? The answer is critical in establishing just when the Rapture takes place. There are a few important prophetic themes that converge and bear upon the answer to this question.

The *first prophetic theme* that bears upon this question has to do with whether the citizens of the Millennial Kingdom are mortals or immortals. The following outline of Scriptures clearly answers that question:

(1) They will bear children (something immortals can't do) (Isaiah 65:20–23; Jeremiah 23:3–6; 30:19–20).

(2) There will be marriage (also a no-no for immortals) (Isaiah 4:1–3).

(3) There will be labor (Isaiah 62:8, 9; 65:21–23; Jeremiah 31:5). One of the first tasks of the

Kingdom citizens will be to clean up the debris of war and bury the dead (Ezekiel 39:9–16).

(4) There will be disobedience and discipline. Even though the Millennial Kingdom begins with only believers, there will be unbelievers among their offspring (Zechariah 14:16–19).

(5) Though longevity will be greatly extended, there will be aging and death (Isaiah 65:20–23).

All of these things are characteristic of mortals, not immortals.

The *second prophetic theme* that relates to this question of who populates the Kingdom concerns *two* great judgments of the Tribulation survivors which takes place on earth immediately after Christ's return. These judgments are the Lord's first major act after returning to the earth.

There is an extremely important condition on earth which is demonstrated by the Lord's judgment of the survivors. These survivors are segregated into two judgments: one of Jews and one of Gentiles. This clearly indicates that the conditions by which God deals with mankind during the Church economy are not operative during the Tribulation. As previously noted, there is no distinction between Jew and Gentile believers in this economy (Galatians 3:27–28; Colossians 3:11). However, the judgments at the end of the Tribulation are completely segregated regardless of whether a Jew or a Gentile is a believer or an unbeliever.

This condition strongly indicates the absence of the Church during the Tribulation, or there would not be this distinction again between Jew and Gentile. These are conditions that prevailed during the time when God's special dealings were with Israel. As I mentioned before, I believe that Old Testament conditions will return when Daniel's Seventieth Week begins. These were in force when this decree was given allotting seventy sabbatical weeks of years for Israel. So since the first sixty-nine weeks of years were under Old Testament conditions, it follows that the Seventieth Week will be too.

The Judgment of Surviving Israelites

Throughout the Old Testament, prophecies were made about the coming of the promised Messianic Kingdom. Many of these spoke of a judgment of the physical descendents of Abraham, Isaac and Jacob to determine who would enter. Paul warned that not all who are called Israel are Israel (Romans 9:6).

Ezekiel clearly forewarned what would immediately precede the Messiah's founding of the Kingdom. In Chapter 20 he said that the Messiah would become king over them with great judgment upon the earth (Verse 33); that He would bring them out of the lands where He had scattered them (Verse 34); that He would bring all living survivors of Israel into the wilderness (probably the Sinai Desert) and judge them face-to-face (Verses 35 and 36); that the judgment would be made according to the covenant He made with them (which demanded faith in His provision for sin) (Verse 37); that He would purge from them all rebels who had transgressed against Him (Verse 38); and that those who remained would be established in the Kingdom (Verses 40–44).

The prophet Zephaniah predicts the same sequence of events. First, he predicts the terrible judgment of the Tribulation (1:14–18); then, the coming of the Lord to earth with great worldwide destruction and judgment (3:8). Next, he predicts a judgment of survivors in which all proud and exulting ones, and all deceitful and lying people, will be removed from their midst (3:11). He also said that only a humble and lowly people who take refuge in the name of the Lord will remain to enter the Kingdom and land of Israel (3:12–13). Finally, the Lord will become the king of Israel and remain in their midst (3:15–17).

These two passages make it very clear that all Jewish survivors will be gathered for judgment "face-to-face" with the Messiah Jesus, and that the believers alone will enter the Messiah's Kingdom.

The Judgment of the Gentile Survivors

After the Lord Jesus judges the Israelites (illustrated by the parables of Matthew 25:1–30), He will then gather all Gentiles to Jerusalem (the place of His glorious throne of Matthew 25:31) and conduct a very personal judgment of all those who survive the Tribulation (Matthew 25:31–46).

This passage very clearly indicates when and upon whom this judgment takes place, "But when the Son of Man comes in His glory, and all the angels with Him, then He will sit on His glorious throne. And all the nations [Gentiles] will be gathered before Him; and He will separate them from one another, as the shepherd separates the sheep [believers] from the goats [unbelievers]; and He will put the sheep on His right, and the goats on the left." (Matthew 25:31–33)

At the end of the judgment and separation the Lord Jesus says, "And these [that is, the goats on the left] will go away into eternal punishment, but the righteous [that is, the sheep on His right] shall go into eternal life."

The word "nations" in Verse 32 should be translated "Gentiles" for two reasons. First, the Greek original *ta ethne* can be translated either way with equal correctness. Second, since those judged are either taken into the Kingdom or cast into eternal judgment, it must be translated "Gentiles," because only individuals can be judged as to eternal destiny. No nation ever has been totally saved or totally lost.

The Lord uses a unique test to determine whether these Tribulation survivors are true believers in Him. This is evaluated on the basis of how they treated a very special group that the Lord Jesus calls "these brothers of mine" (Matthew 25:40, 45). Judging by the unusual survival of this group in spite of hunger, thirst, estrangement, lack of adequate clothing, sickness and imprisonment, it seems certain that they are the 144,000 Jewish witnesses.

They are apparently supernaturally converted just before or at the very beginning of the Tribulation much like the apostle Paul (Revelation 7:1–3). They are separated to Christ in a special way as bond-slaves (*doulos* in Greek) and are sealed with the seal of God. This usually means the indwelling presence of the Holy Spirit (compare 2 Corinthians 1:22; Ephesians 1:13; 4:30).

Because of the salvation report of untold numbers of people from every nation being placed right after the call of the 144,000, it is obvious that the Holy Spirit is indicating the results of their witness (see Revelation 7:9).

At the end of the Tribulation, the same 144,000 are pictured standing with Jesus the Messiah on Mount Zion in Jerusalem (Revelation 14:1–5). The indication is that they all survived the Tribulation and are in *unresurrected* bodies.

Now with that in mind, think of the incredible sufferings these 144,000 evangelists will have to endure. They will be marked men because they are believers from the beginning and preach the message of salvation. They will be hunted, imprisoned, and have no means of economic survival because they will expose the Antichrist and the False Prophet for what they are.

They will have to depend upon their converts to sustain and help them. And since these are going to be men with a price on their heads, only a true believer will risk death to help them. And in the light of Revelation 7:14–17, great numbers of these will be martyred for just such a faith.

But since the 144,000 can't die, they will continue to experience the hunger, thirst and exposure revealed in Revelation 7:16 and Matthew 25:35–40.

So just as Rahab the prostitute proved the genuineness of her faith by helping the Hebrew spies escape from Jericho, so the Tribulation saints will prove theirs by helping the 144,000 evangelists escape the Antichrist.

Finally, with both the unbelieving Israelites and Gentiles removed in judgment, the Kingdom begins with only believers. It is established with justice and righteousness and governed perfectly by the Messiah (Isaiah 11; 65:17–25; Micah 4:1–13). It will last for a thousand years (Revelation 20:4).

THE POST-TRIBULATION ANSWER

With these prophetic themes in mind, let us see how the post-, mid- and pre-Tribulationists answer the question of "Who will populate the Kingdom?"

The *post-Tribulation* view faces the greatest difficulty in answering this question for the following reasons:

(1) The Scriptures specify that only believers who survive the Tribulation will enter the Millennial Kingdom.

(2) Those surviving believers must be mortals with unresurrected bodies.

Yet, as I've said before, in the post-Tribulation scheme for the Rapture, the Rapture occurs simultaneously with the Second Advent of the Lord Jesus at the very end of the Tribulation. Since in the Rapture every living believer on earth will be instantly translated from mortal to immortal, from where will the believing survivors come? The only survivors left in mortal bodies after the Rapture would all be unbelievers.

Furthermore, if the Rapture occurs simultaneously with the Second Advent, how could there be a judgment immediately afterward? The Rapture would have already separated the sheep from the goats. As we have seen, the Lord divides the survivors into two groups. The sheep he calls "the righteous." They have eternal life and enter the Kingdom as mortals. The goats are cast directly into eternal punishment (Matthew 25:46).

Some post-Tribulationists ineffectively try to answer this dilemma by saying that some of the unbelievers will believe immediately after the Rapture, when they see the Lord Jesus returning to the earth. But this is impossible because the basis upon which the Messiah will evaluate genuine faith is determined by how they treated "His brothers" (literally Jesus said, "these brothers of mine" Matthew 25:40) *during the Tribulation.* It is not a "last-second" faith that He speaks of in either Ezekiel 20:33–39 or in Matthew 25:31–46.

The vast majority of post-Tribulationists do not attempt to answer these questions related to who will populate the Kingdom. Most of them do not get into the fine points of the prophetic Scriptures. They rather content themselves with taking potshots at the pre-Tribulationists, contending that pre-Tribulationists base their belief on wishful thinking and hearsay rather than on careful study of the Scriptures. But I'll have more to say about this later. Most of the post-Tribulationists with whom I have had private interaction have not even considered the question discussed in this chapter.

I once had a short debate with Robert Gundry before

the student body at Westmont College. This was sprung on me as a surprise at the end of a series of lectures on prophetic messages I had given for chapel during the spring of 1967. I recall that at that debate I hit Dr. Gundry with the question of who will populate the Kingdom, and he had no answer for it.

This is not the case today though. Gundry is one of those few "post-Tribs" who has wrestled with the fine points of the prophetic system. In his book, published in 1973, Gundry has sought to answer this question.

Gundry believes that the progenitors of the Millennial Kingdom will come from the 144,000. But to arrive at this view, Gundry had to do some fancy allegorical interpretation.

First, Gundry says that the 144,000 evangelists of Revelation Chapters 7 and 14 contain both women and men.[1]

Second, and farther out into the mist of allegorical interpretation, Gundry contends that the 144,000 Israelites are not believers until they see the Lord Jesus coming in the Second Advent. This ingenious but doubtful theory explains how there will be believing Israelites in untranslated bodies still on earth after the Rapture.

Gundry summarizes this view by saying, "Thus, the 144,000 will include both men and women who will populate and replenish the millennial kingdom of Israel. If they resist the Antichrist but remain unbelievers in Christ until the second coming, the reason for their sealing at once becomes apparent: their unconverted state will require special protection from the wrath of God and persecution of the Antichrist."[2]

I reject Gundry's view for the following reasons:

First, it is extremely improbable that the 144,000 con-

---

[1]Robert H. Gundry, *The Church in the Tribulation*, p. 82.
[2]Ibid. pp. 82–83.

tain both women and men. Every noun, pronoun and participle used to refer to them in all the Scriptures is in the masculine gender. Normally, throughout the Bible, men are chosen for such a rugged and hazardous prophetic-evangelistic ministry as is described for the 144,000.

The following reference to the 144,000 also has all the indications of being literal, "These are the ones who have not been defiled with women, for they have kept themselves chaste." (Revelation 14:4a) Although normally there is nothing wrong with having a wife, there are some special ministries where God calls a person to be celibate and totally set apart to his mission (see 1 Corinthians 7:1–7).

Second, I find totally unsupportable the interpretation of the 144,000 being unconverted until the second coming of the Lord Jesus. At the very beginning of the Tribulation, the Bible says, "'Do not harm the earth or the sea or the trees, until we have *sealed* the *bond-servants* of our God on their foreheads.' And I heard the number of those who were *sealed,* one hundred and forty-four thousand *sealed* from every tribe of the sons of Israel." (Revelation 7:3–4)

The term "to seal" (*sphragizo* in Greek) is used throughout the New Testament to refer to the Holy Spirit's presence in a believer in the sense of a sign of God's ownership. This word was used of the imprint made by a signet ring. In those days every person of means had a distinctive symbol in his signet ring. Whenever a person would purchase something, he would press the ring with his seal into wax or clay and attach it to the purchase. That became the sign of his ownership.

Sphragizo is used in Ephesians 1:13 and 14 in the same sense. The Holy Spirit is God's seal within the believer. It is God's pledge that He has purchased us and will bring us to our heavenly home. God's seal upon the 144,000 signifies the same thing.

Gundry's contention that it is to protect them as unbelievers from God's wrath and the Antichrist's persecution doesn't compute. Why would God have to protect chosen ones from His own wrath? And how could they resist the awesome deceptions of the Antichrist, reject his number on pain of death as unbelievers? Unbelievers would not have the motive nor the power source for sustaining such decisions. There will perhaps be some Israelites saved when they see the Messiah coming, but it surely will not be the 144,000 nor the majority of others who are already saved.

Gundry runs into his greatest obstacle in seeking to explain the judgment of the Gentiles at the end of the Tribulation which is predicted in Matthew 25:31–46. This passage presents such formidable problems to the post-Tribulation system that Gundry just seeks to explain it away and wrench it all the way over to the end of the Millennium. I have just shown why the Lord's separating of the believing sheep from the unbelieving goats wouldn't be possible if the Rapture had just occurred.

I believe it is impossible to move this judgment to the end of the Millennium for the following reasons:

First, the overall context of this passage begins in Matthew 24. Jesus first predicted the general signs that would like birth pangs warn of the approach of the Tribulation's beginning (24:1–8); then, He predicts some major events that will occur during the Tribulation's first half (24:9–14); next He predicts major episodes that break forth during the second half of the Tribulation, including the incident that begins it (24:15–28); next He describes the details of His actual return to earth (24:29–31).

There is a break in the consecutive prophetic narrative

at this point. The Lord steps back and gives a parable to apply how the predicted signs were to be understood. He shows that the generation that would see all the signs coming together simultaneously would be the one that would see them all fulfilled (24:32–35).

The Lord Jesus then gave a historical illustration from Noah's day to show that though we would know the general time of His coming (a generation), we would not know the exact time (a day or an hour). I believe that this illustration also shows how the believer from the Church will be taken out before the judgments of the Tribulation fall (24:36–51).

The Lord gives several parables to illustrate specifically how and on what basis the Jews will be judged at the end of the Tribulation (25:1–30). The specifics of this judgment are given in Ezekiel 20:33–38.

The prophetic consecutive narrative continues in Matthew 25:31–46 for the first time since the description of the Lord's return in 24:29–31. The future historical narrative begins again with, "But *when* the Son of Man *comes in his glory,* and all the angels with Him, *then* He will sit on *his glorious throne*." (25:31)

So the context shows that this judgment takes place when Christ comes to earth in His glory and takes His seat on His glorious throne, which is the oft-predicted throne of David in Jerusalem. If Gundry were correct, why would the Lord Jesus come to the earth in His glory at the end of the Millennium? He will have already reigned on this glorious throne for a thousand years.

Second, a formidable obstacle to placing this judgment at the end of the Millennium is the conditions that are described as befalling "His brothers." The Lord speaks of hunger, thirst, nakedness, sickness and imprisonment falling upon those who believe in Him. If Gundry's theory were correct and this judgment occurs at the end of the Millennium, it would be impossible to reconcile such conditions with what the Bible promises concerning the Millennial Kingdom.

For instance, it says there will be no sickness:

"Say to those with palpitating [anxious] hearts, 'Take courage, fear not. Behold your God will come with vengeance . . .' Then the eyes of the blind will be opened, and the ears of the deaf will be unstopped. Then the lame will leap like a deer, the tongue of the dumb will shout for joy . . ." (Isaiah 35:4–6)

"For the youth will die at the age of one hundred, and the one who does not reach the age of one hundred shall be thought accursed." (Isaiah 65:20)

There will be no want for food, drink, shelter or clothes:

"And they shall build houses and inhabit them; they shall also plant vineyards and eat their fruit.

"They shall not build, and another inhabit. They shall not plant, and another eat; for as the lifetime of a tree, so shall be the days of My people, and My chosen ones shall wear out the work of their hands.

"They shall not labor in vain, or bear children for calamity; for they are the offspring of those blessed by the Lord, and their descendents with them." (Isaiah 65:21–23)

There will be no need for prisons because:

(1) Satan will be bound for a thousand years (Revelation 20:2–3).

(2) "They will not hurt or destroy in all My holy mountain, for the earth will be full of the

knowledge of the Lord as the waters cover the sea." (Isaiah 11:9)

(3) "And the Lord will be king over all the earth . . ." (Zechariah 14:9).

(4) "And He will judge between many peoples and render decisions for mighty distant nations. Then they will hammer their swords into plowshares, and their spears into pruning hooks; Nation will not lift up sword against nation, And never again will they train for war. And each of them will sit under his own vine And under his fig tree, With no one to make *them* afraid, For the mouth of the Lord of hosts has spoken." (Micah 4:3–4)

There is no way to move the judgment of Matthew 25:31–46, with its description of horrible human suffering, over to the end of the Millennium. Those sufferings could not happen in the Millennium. This would directly contradict the many promises of the Millennium conditions quoted above.

THE MID-TRIBULATION ANSWER

Most Mid-Tribulationists would have no problem with their system answering who would populate the Kingdom since according to their view, the Rapture occurs at the middle of the Tribulation and many could be saved afterwards.

There is one exception, however. Relfe paints herself into a corner when she says:

"'. . . until the day that *Noah* entered the *ark*, and the *flood* came, and *destroyed them all.*' This was the first great breakthrough in the study! I had never seen this before, although a long time before I had memorized the Scripture! The *day* representing Christ's coming for the church, *Noah* (representing the believer) entered into the *ark* (representing the place prepared for us), the *flood* (representing the wrath of God) came and destroyed them all (representing a doomed world). *Not one person other than Noah and his family was saved.* The remainder of the world immediately received the wrath of God from which there was no escape . . .

"When this great concept was revealed to me, that whenever Christ comes for His Bride, there would be no one else saved, I was *so shaken* by the false teachings of millions saved after the 'catching away'; the multitudes the 144,000 sealed Jews would win, that I literally detached myself from every teaching, doctrine, or belief I had embraced and as a raft in the ocean, I became free to be blown about by the wind of Heaven, the Holy Spirit of God!"[3]

Relfe's dogmatic statement that not one person will be saved after the Mid-Tribulation Rapture makes it impossible for her to answer, "Who will populate the Kingdom?" According to her view, there will only be unbelievers on earth during the last half of the Tribulation and at the Second Coming. Therefore, there would be no need for separating the sheep and goats. They would all be goats, and thus all cast into everlasting punishment.

Furthermore, there could be no Millennium because there would be no mortal believers, nor any mortals for that matter, left to enter the Kingdom.

Relfe's major premise for establishing her mid-Tribulation view is that the wrath of God only falls upon the

[3]Mary Stewart Relfe, *When Your Money Fails*, pp. 190–191.

second half of the Tribulation, not the first. As I indicated earlier the wrath of God falls on man primarily in the spiritual realm in the first half of the Tribulation, and in the physical realm in the second half. We aren't to believe that God's wrath is expressed only in physical judgments, are we? Indeed, the terrible judgments that God sends upon the world through the unrestrained, deceptive miracles of Satan are far worse because they will send men's souls to hell forever (2 Thessalonians 2:9–13).

God will deliver us from both His wrath in the spiritual and the physical sphere because He will come for us before the Tribulation begins.

My spirit was grieved with some of the statements Relfe made, such as, "And now, Brothers and Sisters in Christ, some of the things I have written in prior chapters, I honestly confessed were 'prudent assessments.' I must now make a radical departure and commend to you that which is contained in this chapter relevant to the overall structure of Daniel's Seventieth Week is Divine Revelation! The same Holy Ghost who moved Holy men of old to 'write the things that shall be hereafter' moved on me divinely revealing to me what it was He originally spoke to them!

". . . Finally brethren, I am aware that the hour has come; and that God has indeed 'brought me to the Kingdom for just such a time as this' and to this very chapter in which I boldly confess that I come to you in the role of a New Testament 'Prophet.'"[4]

There is no question but what Mrs. Relfe is sincere. But to claim that the Lord appeared to her and told her that her mid-Tribulation view was correct is treading onto dangerous ground. All I can say is that we all need to "try the spirits to see whether they are from God." (1 John 4:1)

[4]Ibid. pp. 185–186.

THE PRE-TRIBULATION ANSWER

The pre-Tribulation view has no problem answering who will populate the Kingdom. Nor does it have a problem harmonizing the judgments at the end of the Tribulation.

(1) The Lord will Rapture the Church believers before the beginning of Daniel's Seventieth Week.

(2) The Antichrist will be revealed and will take over the ten-nation confederacy of Europe.

(3) He will sign a covenant with the leader of Israel, the False Prophet, which begins Daniel's Seventieth Week.

(4) Around this same time, God will send the two prophets (Moses and Elijah), and will seal the 144,000 evangelists.

(5) They will have a great harvest of souls, although most will be martyred (Revelation 7:9–17). Incidentally, God says these martyrs are killed during "the great Tribulation," which is the second half of Daniel's final week (Revelation 7:14). (This also disproves Relfe's contention that no one will be saved during the "Great Tribulation.")

(6) The Lord returns to earth and judges the Jewish and Gentile survivors separately.

(7) The believers of both groups go into the Kingdom, and the unbelievers to eternal punishment.

PTL

As I close this chapter, my soul praises the Lord for His grace that has given us a sure hope for the living and not the dead. Believers from the Church will enter the Millennial Kingdom, but in immortal bodies as priests and corulers with the Lord Jesus. And dear brothers and sisters, that's grace!

ELEVEN

THE RESURRECTIONS IN REVIEW

There are two categories of resurrection in the Bible. One is only for believers who have died, and is called "the resurrection of life" (John 5:29). The other category of resurrection is for all unbelievers of all dispensations, and is called "the resurrection of damnation" (John 5:29, KJV).

There is a strong disagreement between pre- and post-Tribulationists concerning the resurrection of life, or as it is also called, "the first resurrection" (Revelation 20:4–6). The disagreement concerns whether the first resurrection occurs only at the end of the Tribulation (which is the post-Tribulation view), or whether it takes place in several stages at different points of history (the view of pre-Tribulationists and some mid-Tribulationists).

If the post-Tribulationists could prove that there is only one phase to the resurrection of life, and that it occurs at the Second Coming, then they could make a strong case against pre- and mid-Tribulationism. The reason is because there is a resurrection and a translation of saints at the Rapture. If the Rapture is separated by seven years from the Second Coming, as pre-Tribulationists contend, then there has to be at least one more phase in order to resurrect the Old Testament and Tribulation saints. Daniel 12:1–3 clearly places the resurrection of Old Testament saints at the end of the Tribulation. And Revelation 20:1–5 definitely places the resurrection of Tribulation saints **after** the Lord Jesus comes to earth, judges the Antichrist, binds Satan and judges the living survivors.

All seem to agree about "the resurrection of damnation" which raises only unbelievers from the dead in bodies of corruption. This resurrection takes place at the end of time when all unbelievers from every dispensation will be raised to stand judgment at the Great White Throne (Revelation 20:11–15).

The First Resurrection—Several Stages

Paul flatly states that the first resurrection has at least three stages:

Stage one was the resurrection of the Lord Jesus the Messiah. Paul says, "But now Christ has been raised from the dead, the first fruits of those who are asleep." (1 Corinthians 15:20)

Stage two will be the resurrection of at least the believers of the present economy of grace. Paul says again, "But each in his own order: Christ the first fruits, after that *those who are Christ's at His coming* . . ." (1 Corinthians 15:23).

Stage three will be at the end of the Millennium when time ends and eternity begins. It is at that point that death is abolished. Believers who are alive at the end of the Kingdom economy will be translated from mortal to immortal. This is all implied by the statement, "The last enemy that will be abolished is death." (1 Corinthians 15:26)

Gundry disagrees with this, of course. But he does make some interesting statements: "The first resurrection does in fact take place in phases. But only *two* phases of the resurrection can be determined from clear and specific chronological notations . . . *In principle we should not consider a pretribulational phase of the first resurrection impossible*, but we need scriptural evidence."[1] (Emphasis mine.)

I deeply appreciate this honest statement. Now let's look at some Scriptural evidence. As stated above, there are at least three stages, not just two, indicated in 1 Corinthians Chapter 15.

The Different Battalions of Resurrection

The apostle Paul uses an extremely important term in relation to the stages of resurrection. He says again, "But each in his *order* . . ." (1 Corinthians 15:23a). *"Order"* is the translation of the Greek word *tagma* which was primarily a military term. It was most frequently used to designate a division or battalion of soldiers. The best available Greek New Testament lexicon says about this term, "Of a number of persons who belong together and are therefore arranged together; *division; group.* A military term for bodies of troops in various numbers such as divisions or battalions of soldiers . . . in 1 Corinthians 15:23f the gift of life is given to various ones in turn, and at various times. One view is that in this connection Paul distinguishes three groups: Christ, who already possesses life, the Christians, who will receive it at His second coming, and the rest of humanity, who will receive it when death, the last of God's enemies, is destroyed."[2]

[1]Robert H. Gundry, *The Church and the Tribulation*, p. 148.
[2]F. W. Gingrich and Frederick Danker, *A Greek-English Lexicon of the New Testament*, p. 802.

Paul paints a word picture which describes army divisions on parade passing by a reviewing stand at different intervals in time. Even so, the believers are to be resurrected, but each one in **his own division.** The very term, *tagma*, implies a number of phases.

Precedents for Many Phases

There are some very unusual incidences of resurrection which at the very least establish a precedent for having more than two phases within the "resurrection of life."

The *first case* occurred shortly after the Lord Jesus was raised from the dead. The Word of God says, "And the tombs were opened; and *many* bodies of the saints who had fallen asleep *were raised;* and coming out of the tombs after His [Jesus'] resurrection they entered the holy city and appeared to many." (Matthew 27:52–53) This verse definitely indicates that a token number of saints who had recently died were resurrected at the time of Jesus' resurrection.

This group very much resembles the wave sheaf offering that was part of the first fruits of the Divinely ordained schedule within Israel's harvest season. When the first of the grain was harvested, they celebrated the feast of the first fruits (Exodus 23:16). Concerning this, God said to Moses, "Speak to the sons of Israel, and say to them, 'When you enter the land which I am going to give to you and reap its harvest, then you shall bring in the sheaf of the first fruits of your harvest to the priest. And he shall wave the sheaf before the Lord for you to be accepted . . .'" (Leviticus 23:10–11).

The priest waved this bundle of grain tied together from the first fruits (the wave sheaf) before the Lord inside the holy place of the tabernacle of worship. This demonstrated both Israel's thankfulness and their faith in God for a full and bountiful harvest to come.

I believe that this was a beautiful expression of the resurrection. The fact that Jesus is called "the first fruits of those who sleep" certainly authorizes the analogy. For Jesus is both the first fruits and our great High Priest. He took the wave sheaf of believers resurrected with Him and waved them before the Lord in the heavenly tabernacle. He thus expressed faith for us of a certain and bountiful harvest in the future. Just as the wave sheaf was only accepted with a sacrificed lamb, so the Lord Jesus, our Lamb, made the wave sheaf of man's resurrection acceptable. This wave sheaf was a guarantee of our resurrection.

Israel's harvest had many phases. The first fruits and wave sheaf was first. The main harvest was next. Then there was another phase at the end of the harvest called "the Feast of the Ingathering" (Exodus 23:16). Afterwards, the *gleanings* were harvested by the alien and needy in Israel (Leviticus 23:22). The following chart illustrates how Israel's harvest could be a type of the various stages of the first resurrection.

The *second case* that sets a precedent is the future resurrection of the two Old Testament prophets who are sent back to prophesy in Jerusalem for the first three and one-half years of the Tribulation. In the middle of the Tribulation, when unlimited authority is given to the Antichrist (Revelation 13:5–8), he will kill the two prophets (Revelation 11:4–10). Their dead bodies will be exposed to the world in the streets of Jerusalem for three and one-half days. Then, the Scripture says, "And after the three days and a half the breath of life from God came into them, and they stood on their feet; and great fear fell upon those who were beholding them. And they heard a loud noise from heaven saying to them, 'Come up here.' And they went up into heaven in the cloud, and their enemies beheld them." (Revelation 11:11–12)

**ORDER OF RESURRECTION
PRE-TRIBULATION RAPTURE**

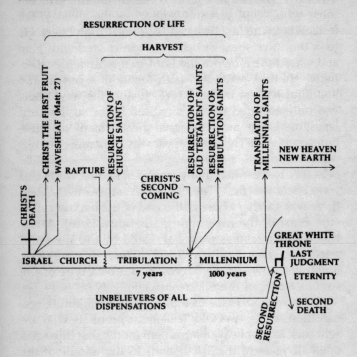

The whole world will probably see this by satellite television. We now have the technical ability to fulfill what is predicted, "And those from the peoples and tribes and tongues and nations will *look* at their dead bodies for three days and a half, and will not permit their dead bodies to be laid in a tomb." (Revelation 11:9)

Gundry objects to this scenario. He makes a big point of the fact that the Scriptures nowhere mention a resurrection of the Church prior to the Tribulation. But then the Scriptures nowhere specifically mention the resurrection of the Church at the middle or the end of the Tribulation either.

The resurrection of the Tribulation saints is mentioned as occurring *after* the second coming (Revelation 20:1–6).

There is no way to escape the chronology of the Tribulation saints' resurrection. According to 20:4, it occurs after the Lord Jesus returns and sets up thrones of judgment on earth.

That does not fit with Gundry's post-Tribulational chronology either. His sequence of events requires the Church to be resurrected just **before** the second coming. So like it or not, there is still a gap of time between the Church's resurrection and that of the Tribulation saints even in the post-Tribulational scheme.

All premillennialists, whether pre-, mid-, or post-Tribulationist, have a bit of a problem with exactly how the saints of the Millennial Kingdom get from mortal bodies to immortal ones. This is so because the Scripture says, "The rest of the dead did not come to life until the thousand years were completed. This is the first resurrection. Blessed and holy is the one who has part in the first resurrection; over these the second death has no power, but they will be priests of God and of Christ and will reign with Him for a thousand years." (Revelation 20:5–6)

These verses seem to indicate that the first resurrection, the one of life, will end with the resurrection of the saints at the end of the Tribulation. In view of this, what happens to the mortal believers at the end of the Millennium?

One good explanation is that only unbelievers who are a menace to society will die. The initial believing parents who start the Millennial Kingdom will have some children who will not believe. This is why it is predicted that the Messiah Jesus will rule the nations with a rod of iron. Isaiah's prophecy supports the theory that only unbelievers will die, ". . . the one who does not reach the age of one hundred shall be *thought* accursed" (Isaiah 65:20b). The accursed one who dies would be the unbeliever who disrupts society.

Another statement indicates that believers will live through the entire thousand years. Isaiah said not only that a person would be a child at one hundred years of age, but he also predicted that the Kingdom saints' days would be as the lifetime of a tree (Isaiah 65:22). I know of some trees that are more than two thousand years old.

If this explanation is correct, and I think that it is, then the only resurrection that would need to take place at the end of the Millennium is the one of damnation. The millennial saints would be translated directly into immortality when death is abolished. (1 Corinthians 15:26)

CONCLUSIONS

We have seen how the first resurrection must have more than one phase. Even if the post-Tribulationists could prove the Rapture occurs at the beginning of Christ's return to earth (which they cannot), they still couldn't answer the problem of the resurrection of Tribulation saints which occurs after Christ has returned and judged the earth (Revelation 19:19–20:6).

Relfe, who I found to be a very unorthodox mid-Tribulationist, arrogantly paints herself into another theological corner, "Now, in an attempt to clarify a few other classic errors being propagated, let me summarize some of my findings: The pre-Tribulation Theory has *no resurrection*! The first resurrection of Revelation 20:4–6 is the only resurrection for the just, for the only coming of Christ for the church. (His coming back to the earth is *with all* the saints.) (Zechariah 14:5). Many have manufactured aberrations of the scripture teaching first fruits, gleanings, and harvesting resurrections. Hear therefore, what the scriptures say . . . ," and so on and so forth.[3]

Relfe's statement and following argument in her book are a bit hard to follow, but the essence is this: There is only one resurrection of the just. There are no phases or successive stages within it. The one resurrection of the just occurs at the last trumpet which she identifies as the end of the Tribulation.

This argument truly startled me because Relfe said that the Lord appeared to her on different occasions and told her that He was coming in the middle of the Tribulation. Yet, the clear meaning of the above argument is *a post-Tribulation* Rapture. Because if there is only one phase of the resurrection of the just, then the resurrection that precedes the translation of the Rapture couldn't take place in mid-Tribulation.

I believe that there are several stages to the resurrection . . . and one of them is about to happen!

[3]Mary Stewart Relfe, *When Your Money Fails*, p. 200.

TWELVE

THE PROPHETIC BOOKS UNSEALED

"But as for you, Daniel, **conceal** these words and **seal up** the book **until the end time**; many will go back and forth, and knowledge will increase.

"As for me, I heard but could not understand; so I said, 'My lord, what will be the outcome of these events?' And he said, 'Go your way, Daniel, for these words are **concealed** and **sealed up until the end time**. Many will be purged, purified and refined; but the wicked will act wickedly, and none of the wicked will understand, but those who have insight [who are wise] **will understand**.'" (Daniel 12:4, 8–10)

Frankly, I have become a bit bored with those *nouveau* post-Tribulationists who give the impression that if you were truly an intellectual and *macho Christian*, you would charge headlong with them into the Tribulation.

And I am amazed that some of the older post-Tribulationists like Alexander Reese, George Ladd and Robert

Gundry spend an inordinate amount of time and energy trying to prove the recent origins of the pre-Tribulation view. Ladd devotes almost a third of his book to this point.[1] Some never tire of tracing the whole original concept of the pre-Tribulation Rapture back to 1830 and a young Scottish girl named Margaret Macdonald, to another Scotsman, Edward Irving, and an Englishman named John Darby.

More will be said about this in a moment, but my main point here is that even if this could all be proven, so what?

The Roman Catholic Church used the same kind of method of reasoning against Martin Luther, John Calvin and the other theologians of the Reformation. They brought up more than a thousand years of Church tradition and institutional Bible interpretation against the reformers' *new* doctrine of justification by faith alone. The Church also quoted a majority of the so-called Church fathers from the second through the fifth centuries who believed in salvation by faith *plus* works. But did that disprove what the Scriptures said? Didn't this rather show that traditional interpretation can sometimes miss a truth that is nevertheless contained in the Scriptures?

Another surprising method of attack used by many post-Tribulationists against the pre-Tribulation position is to list a number of impressive theologians who hold the post-Tribulation view. There is no question that there have been and still are godly, scholarly and effective men of God who hold this view. But does that really prove anything? Can't pre-Tribulationists make their own list of adherents which is at least as impressive? What are we going to say: My godly scholars are more godly and scholarly than yours? Such arguments prove nothing.

[1]George Eldon Ladd, *The Blessed Hope*.

The real issue of eschatology (prophecy of last days) is that God through Daniel clearly forewarned that the book of prophecy would be "concealed and sealed" until the time of fulfillment began to draw near. So what in fact has happened in the historical development of theology should be no surprise. Although every other doctrine of the Bible was progressively and systematically defined, eschatology was the last.

A SHORT HISTORY OF PROPHETIC INTERPRETATION

The first century Church held an undefined faith in the 'any moment' possibility of Christ's return, called the doctrine of imminence. It also believed in a literal thousand-year reign of Christ on earth after the Second Advent, called premillennialism.

Prophecy's Dark Ages

The influential early Church leader, Augustine (A.D. 354–430) dealt the doctrine of prophecy the most damaging blow of anyone in history. He plunged the study of prophecy into darkness for almost 1,400 years by systematically teaching that prophecy could not be interpreted literally.

Augustine held to a literal, grammatical and historical interpretation of every other field of Bible doctrine, but taught that prophecy must be interpreted allegorically. He did this in order to be able to sustain his views of the Church, which he set forth in a profound book called *The City of God*. This book dominated the thinking of the Church for hundreds of years afterward.

Augustine taught that the Church had taken Israel's place, and had been given the promises and covenants which (in this view) Israel had forfeited by rejecting

Christ. He taught that the Church is the Kingdom of God in an allegorical sense, and that there would be no literal future 1,000-year earthly kingdom over which Christ would reign. (Amillennialism began here.) He taught that the Church should rule the world even in a political sense (as the Millennial Kingdom will rule in the future).

Augustine's Influence

Augustine's views became the foundation upon which the Roman Catholic Church was built. It still holds most of his views.

Augustine's teachings also became the philosophical basis for "Christian" anti-Semitism. He taught that Jews had no more purpose in God's plan; that they would never be reborn as a nation; that the covenants were no longer valid to them; that they were spiritual castaways with no future hope, Christ-killers who had no more place in God's plan and imposters. (All this, as strange as it may sound, was the result of a method of interpreting prophetic passages in an allegorical sense. Let me emphasize again, no one who interprets prophecy literally, as Jesus Himself and the apostles interpreted Old Testament prophecies in the New Testament, could ever fall into Satan's anti-Semitic trap.)

The Period of Prophetic Ferment

When the Reformers broke away from the Roman Church in the early sixteenth century, they retained Augustine's allegorical, amillennial view of prophecy.

For the next 250 years, reformed theologians began to reexamine all areas of systematic theology. It was during this period, when Protestants were dividing into many denominations with divergent views about amillennialism, that a new view, postmillennialism, emerged.

This view taught that the Church would eventually convert the whole world through the preaching of the Gospel. This would usher in the golden age promised for the Millennial Kingdom. They believed the Church would rule the world for a thousand years. Christ would then return and take the Church into eternity. Liberals at this time even accepted Darwin's theory of evolution, with all its optimism, as God's method of ushering in the "golden age." More conservative post- and amillennarian theologians recognized this as a departure from the faith and attempted to combat the theory. This was one of the reasons for the rise of the many prophetic conferences of the last century. Augustine's nonliteral interpretation of prophecy was called into question. Premillennialism emerged, claiming to return to the early Church's prophetic view and method of prophetic interpretation.[2]

From the time of Augustine until the early nineteenth century, the traditional church's interpretation of prophecy did not allow for the possibility of a literal 1,000-year Kingdom, a literal Tribulation, *or* a Rapture that was distinguished from the Second Advent. In their view, the Church was already in the "Tribulation," so it stands to reason that they would hold to a post-Tribulation coming of Christ.

The return to a literal, grammatical, historical interpretation of prophecy during the early nineteenth century called for a thorough redefining of systematic eschatology for the first time in history. It was in this larger historical context that the whole controversy concerning the Rapture began. To say that the controversy started with the single vision of a fifteen-year-old Scottish girl is patently ridiculous.

Because there has been so much made of this girl's vision, I am going to quote it in its entirety.

The following is Margaret Macdonald's account of her vision which was received in 1830. This is taken from Robert Norton's publication, *Memoirs of James and George Macdonald, of Port-Glasgow* (1840).

"It was first the awful state of the land that was pressed upon me. I saw the blindness and infatuation of the people to be very great. I felt the cry of Liberty just to be the hiss of the serpent, to drown them in perdition. It was just 'no God.' I repeated the words, Now there is distress of nations, with perplexity, the seas and the waves roaring, men's hearts failing them for fear—now look out for the sign of the Son of man. Here I was made to stop and cry out, O it is not known what the sign of the Son of man is; the people of God think they are waiting, but they know not what it is. I felt this needed to be revealed, and that there was great darkness and error about it; but suddenly what it was burst upon me with a glorious light. I saw it was just the Lord himself descending from Heaven with a shout, just the glorified man, even Jesus; but that all must, as Stephen was, be filled with the Holy Ghost, that they might look up, and see the brightness of the Father's glory. I saw the error to be, that men think that it will be something seen by the natural eye; but 'tis spiritual discernment that is needed, the eye of God in his people. Many passages were revealed, in a light in which I had not before seen them. I repeated, 'Now is the kingdom of Heaven like unto ten virgins, who went forth to meet the Bridegroom, five wise and five foolish; they that were foolish took their lamps, but took no oil with them, but they that were wise took oil in their vessels with their lamps.' 'But be ye not unwise, but understanding what the will of the Lord is; and be not drunk with wine wherein is excess, but be filled with the Spirit.' This was the oil the wise virgins took in their vessels—this is the light to be kept burning—the light of God—that we may discern that which cometh not with observation to the natural eye. Only those who have the light of God within them will see the sign of his appearance. No need to follow them who say, see here, or see there, for his day shall be as the lightning to those in whom the living Christ is. 'Tis Christ in us that will lift us up—he is the light—'tis only those that are alive in him that will be caught up to meet him in the air. I saw that we must be in the Spirit, that we might see spiritual things. John was in the Spirit, when he saw a throne set in Heaven.—But I saw that the glory of the ministration of the Spirit had not been known. I repeated frequently, but the spiritual temple must and shall be reared, and the fulness of Christ be poured into his body, and then shall we be caught up to meet him. Oh none will be counted worthy of this calling but his body, which is the church, and which must be a candlestick all of gold. I often said, Oh the glorious inbreaking of God which is now about to burst on this earth; Oh the glorious temple which is now about to be reared, the bride adorned for her husband; and Oh what a holy, holy bride she must be, to be prepared for such a glorious bridegroom. I said, Now shall the people of God have to do with realities—now shall the glorious mystery of God in our nature be known—now shall it be known what it is for man to be glorified. I felt that the revelation of Jesus Christ had yet to be opened up—it is not knowledge about God that it contains, but it is an entering into God—I saw that there was a glorious breaking in of God to be. I felt as Elijah, surrounded with chariots of fire. I saw as it were, the spiritual temple reared, and the Head Stone brought forth with shoutings of grace, grace, unto it. It was a glorious light above the brightness of the sun, that shown round about me. I felt that those who were filled with the Spirit could see spiritual things, and feel walking in the midst of them, while those who had not the Spirit could see nothing—so that two shall be in one bed, the one taken and other left, because the one has the light of God within while the other cannot see the Kingdom of Heaven. I saw the people of God in an awfully dangerous situation, surrounded by nets and entanglements, about to be tried, and many about to be deceived and fall. Now will **the wicked** be revealed, with all power and signs and lying wonders, so that if it were possible the very elect will be deceived.—This is the fiery trial which is to try us.—It will be for the purging and purifying of the real members of the body of Jesus; but Oh it will be a fiery trial. Every soul will be shaken to the very centre. The enemy will try to shake in every thing we have believed—but the trial of real faith will be found to honour and praise and glory. Nothing but what is of God will stand. The stony-ground hearers will be made manifest—the love of many will wax cold. I frequently said that night, and often since, now shall the awful sight of a false Christ be seen on this earth, and nothing but the living Christ in us can detect this awful attempt of the enemy to deceive—for it is with all deceivableness of unrighteousness he will work— he will have a counterpart for every part of God's truth, and an imitation for every work of the Spirit. The Spirit must and will be poured out on the Church, that she may be purified and filled with God—and just in proportion as the Spirit of God works, so will he—when our Lord anoints men with power, so will he. This is particularly the nature of the trial, through which those are to pass who will be counted worthy to stand before the Son of man. There

will be outward trial too, but 'tis principally
temptation. It is brought on by the outpouring of the
Spirit, and will just increase in proportion as the Spirit
is poured out. The trial of the Church is from
Antichrist. It is by being filled with the Spirit that we
shall be kept. I frequently said, Oh be filled with the
Spirit—have the light of God in you, that you may
detect satan—be full of eyes within—be clay in the
hands of the potter—submit to be filled, filled with
God. This will build the temple. It is not by might nor
by power, but by my Spirit, saith the Lord. This will
fit us to enter into the marriage supper of the Lamb. I
saw it to be the will of God that all should be filled.
But what hindered the real life of God from being
received by his people, was their turning from Jesus,
who is the way to the Father. They were not entering
in by the door. For he is faithful who hath said, by me
if any man enter in he shall find pasture. They were
passing the cross, through which every drop of the
Spirit of God flows to us. All power that comes not
through the blood of Christ is not of God. When I say,
they are looking from the cross, I feel that there is
much in it—they turn from the blood of the Lamb, by
which we overcome, and in which our robes are
washed and made white. There are low views of
God's holiness, and a ceasing to condemn sin in the
flesh, and a looking from him who humbled himself,
and made himself of no reputation. Oh! It is needed,
much needed at present, a leading back to the cross. I
saw that night, and often since, that there will be an
outpouring of the Spirit on the body, such as has not
been, a baptism of fire, that all the dross may be put
away. Oh there must and will be such an indwelling of
the living God as has not been—the servants of God
sealed in their foreheads—great conformity to Jesus—
just the bride made comely, by his comeliness put

upon her. This is what we are at present made to pray much for, that speedily we may all be made ready to meet our Lord in the air—and it will be. Jesus wants his bride. His desire is toward us. He that shall come, will come, and will not tarry. Amen and Amen. Even so come Lord Jesus."

Some Observations

How anyone with a straight face can say that this vision is the origin of the whole pre-Tribulation view is beyond me. The following are a few observations on what it teaches:

(1) She definitely teaches *a partial Rapture*. The spiritual Christians are to be removed and the unspiritual remain to go through fiery trials.

(2) She taught that even the spiritual ones would be on earth during the Antichrist's (The Wicked One) period of terrible deceptions. This means that the "spiritual Christians" would at least go through half of the Tribulation.

(3) She equates "the sign of the Son of man" from Matthew 24:30 (which is referring to the Second Advent) with the Rapture statement of 1 Thessalonians 4:16, "The Lord Himself will descend from heaven with a shout." She says they occur at the same time. Even Dave Mac-Pherson acknowledges this.[3] In spite of what others may say, this makes her view of the Rapture post-Tribulational.

The Snow Job

MacPherson and others have sought to disprove pre-Tribulationism by tracing it to this vision. But the very

[3] *The Incredible Cover-Up* by Omega Publications, p. 154.

evidence MacPherson quotes proves the exact opposite of what he claims it teaches.

Furthermore, to say that John Darby, who was adamantly against the charismatic gifts, got his insight into prophecy from Margaret Macdonald is incredible and unprovable. Margaret Macdonald herself doesn't seem to have made much of her vision. In fact, there's very little recorded about it.[4]

It is possible that Darby was not aware of it, for he never mentions it, though he does write concerning her.[5] But even if he had been aware of it, it really makes no difference, for her views are not only different but contradictory to what Darby believed. To portray Darby as a plagiarist, eager to take all the glory, is to slander a brother in the Lord with no evidence. There's also no reason to believe that a careful scholar like Darby would allow himself to be influenced by the vision of a young, unschooled girl, since he didn't believe in her gift to begin with.

From all we can gather of the times, John Darby was a Biblical scholar who was simply a part of the wave of new interest in prophecy. The return to literal interpretation of prophecy led him and others to begin to redefine prophecy, and to arrange it into a cohesive system.

So What?

The most important factor in this whole controversy is, "What does the Bible say?" I totally agree with Ladd when he said, "Let it be at once emphasized that we are

[4]I'd like to say that although I don't agree with the authenticity of her vision, records show her to be a beautiful sister in the Lord, filled with love and compassion for others.

[5]In Darby's book, *The Irrationalism of Infidelity* (1853) he speaks of Margaret Macdonald and her two brothers, disputing the authenticity of their gift of tongues.

not turning to the church fathers to find authority for either pre- or post-Tribulationism. The one authority is the Word of God, and we are not confined in the strait-jacket of tradition."[6] All I can say is "amen" to that statement.

As I stated at the beginning of this study, my purpose for writing this book was not to cling blindly to a system of prophetic interpretation, but rather to objectively and honestly investigate what the whole Bible says.

In closing this book I can say in all good conscience that I believe the Scriptures teach a pre-Tribulational coming of the Lord Jesus Christ for His Church.

No matter which view one holds on the Rapture questions, there are some difficult problems that have to be reconciled within the system. I believe that the pre-Tribulation system answers all the Scriptures on the subject in the most consistent and harmonious way.

On the other hand, the post-Tribulation system has to allegorize some major portions of the Scripture, such as Matthew 25:31–46 and the question of who will populate the Kingdom, in order to make their system work.

Second, the major assumption of many of the post-Tribulationists' arguments is that if they can punch holes in the pre-Trib system, it somehow establishes their own.

What is said about the post-Tribulationists also applies to the Mid-Tribulation view.

ON A PERSONAL NOTE

I have never been more thankful to God for the personal hope of the Lord's return for the believer before the coming world holocaust. I had unwittingly begun to take this wonderful truth for granted.

[6]Ladd, op. cit. p. 19.

It breaks my heart as I daily pore over world events and see how rapidly the world as we know it is moving toward a catastrophic end.

—Experts say that we are headed for a global economic collapse. Third world countries keep piling up massive debts. They can't even pay interest, much less principal on their loans.

—Many jobs lost in the latest recession will never be restored—experts speak of a whole generation being unemployable because of the painful change from the industrial age to a new technical age of uncertain destiny.

—The Arab-Israeli conflict continues to smolder with the constant threat of igniting the fuse of Armageddon.

—The Soviet Union, already the mightiest military power in history, continues to move in all parts of the globe and wear down the will of the free world to resist.

—Nuclear weapons capable of destroying all life on earth continue to be produced at the rate of approximately six warheads per week.

—"Star Wars" type technology rapidly moves toward lasers and deathrays of unimaginable lethality.

—China, with more than one-fourth of the world's population, continues to prepare for war.

—Global weather patterns continue to change—storms of unusual force strike in new places.

—Lawlessness is rampant

  • murders continue to increase—no city is safe;

  • gang rapes occur while average citizens look on and cheer;

- jails are filled to overcapacity with criminals of all kinds;

- drugs are virtually a staple of the modern society;

- family units are almost nonexistent;

- bizarre murders with no motive are commonplace.

—Famines continue to expand over large sections of the world's population.

—Volcanoes, long dormant, explode.

—Earthquakes continue to increase in frequency and severity.

To the untrained eye, this may sound like unrelated bad news. But to the student of prophecy, it all fits into a precise pattern that was forecast long ago. This pattern clearly shows us that the Lord's coming for the Church is very near.

The hope of the Rapture is a very practical force in my life at this point in history. It motivates me to gain a combat knowledge of the Bible in order to be able to face the perilous times that precede the Tribulation. It motivates me to win as many to Christ as possible before it's too late. I want to take as many with me as I can. Although I grieve over the lost world that is headed toward catastrophe, the hope of the Rapture keeps me from despair in the midst of ever-worsening world conditions.

The one who knows that Jesus Christ is in his heart and has the sure hope of the Lord's coming for him before the Tribulation is the only one who can face today's news and honestly be optimistic.

My prayer is that this book has helped you to have a certain and sure hope of the Lord's "any moment" return to take you to His Father's house.

I'll see you at His feet!

HAL LINDSEY

ABOUT THE AUTHOR

HAL LINDSEY, named *the bestselling author of the decade* by the New York Times, was born in Houston, Texas. His first book, *The Late Great Planet Earth,* published in 1970, became the bestselling non-fiction book of the decade, selling more than 18 million copies worldwide. He is one of the few authors to have three books on the New York Times bestseller list at the same time.

Mr. Lindsey was educated at the University of Houston. After serving in the U.S. Coast Guard during the Korean War, Mr. Lindsey graduated from Dallas Theological Seminary where he majored in the New Testament and early Greek literature. After completing seminary, Mr. Lindsey served for eight years on the staff of Campus Crusade for Christ, speaking to tens of thousands of students on major university campuses throughout the United States.

If you wish to order tapes of messages by the author, write:

Hal Lindsey Ministries
P.O. Box 7000-06
Palos Verdes, CA   90274

HAL LINDSEY

Here are other all-time bestsellers from the author whose biblical prophesies and startling revelations about the world and mankind have given him a following of millions of devoted readers.

Prices and availability subject to change without notice.

Heartwarming Books
of
Faith and Inspiration